WARRIOR BARD

EDWARD AND STEPHANI GODWIN

WARRIOR BARD

*

THE LIFE OF
WILLIAM MORRIS

ILLUSTRATED BY THE AUTHORS

KENNIKAT PRESS
Port Washington, N. Y./London

WARRIOR BARD

First published in 1947
Reissued in 1970 by Kennikat Press
Library of Congress Catalog Card No: 70-103190
SBN 8046-0827-X

Manufactured by Taylor Publishing Company   Dallas, Texas

PRELUDE

TO study the ideals of William Morris is now more than ever necessary if we are to gain the truly Socialistic life which we all want. This life does not consist of *panem et circenses*—high wages paid in inflated coin, cinemas, football pools, chain-smoking, news propaganda. It consists, rather, in every one's taking an active and intelligent part in the general progress of humanity. In this new world it will be no longer possible for an unscrupulous minority to pass off Dictatorship as Socialism, drugging the mass of mankind into obedience by pandering to its lowest tastes, while purposely withholding everything that should make it wiser, healthier, and happier. In this new world founded on Commonwealth every one of us will have an honourable and necessary place, truly independent and truly free.

In spite of the attempts of one or two would-be fashionable writers to make a hit by holding up such subjects as the Pre-Raphaelites to scandal or ridicule, including William Morris and his wife as Victorian jokes, people who have any knowledge of the subject know that Morris was not a Pre-Raphaelite, but was—besides being one of England's greatest writers and designers—the most clear-sighted sociologist of his age, gifted with an understanding absolutely independent of century, nationality, or class. And it is for those who wish for accurate information based on sound and disinterested scholarship, realizing that the teachings of William Morris can give them something of vital value in facing life to-day, that this book has been written.

We often discussed with our old friend Miss May Morris our idea of making the life of her father into a really vivid story. Miss Morris strongly approved, and towards the end of her life gave us many intimate anecdotes and personal reminis-cences which would otherwise have never become known to the world.

And so we can take you back to walk beside him, hear him, know him, as some one most real and living. You will feel, when you close this book, that you have met a great and wonderful personality, and that the meeting, though brief, is going to leave its impression on the whole of your life and thought. Few of us have the good fortune to come into contact with the truly great of the world, but all who read this book will be able to carry with them to the end of their days the impression that they have met and known that great warrior bard William Morris.

May this impression be like the seed that falls on good ground.

E. G.
S. G.

ACKNOWLEDGMENT

WE should like to take this opportunity of thanking Mr G. A. Evans for the great help which he gave us in carrying out the research work which was necessary for the chapters dealing with the Marlborough period of Morris's life; also of acknowledging the debt to Dr J. W. Mackail which all who study Morris must incur.

Our other sources of information are too numerous to mention here; the use of innumerable private letters, note-books, journals, as well as daily contact with some who served Morris and his family, has been our privilege as tenants of Kelmscott Manor, William Morris's country home, and guardians of the Art Collection which Miss Morris left there.

E. G.
S. G.

Kelmscott Manor
  Lechlade
    Gloucestershire

April 1947

To Starlight
and the Memory of May Morris

CONTENTS

The initials indicate authorship of the chapters.

Chapter 1

THE WARRIOR

To this day the smell of may always reminds me of going to bed
by daylight.

Quoted by J. W. Mackail as a saying of William Morris

THE first sunbeams had scarcely begun to glance greenly
into the hornbeam depths of Epping Forest, or sparkle
on the little river Roding that ran near by, when a
small, sturdy figure in shining armour came galloping out of
the forest shouting and waving a sword.

It was young William Morris out riding by himself, in a
suit of toy armour given to him on the 24th of March, his eighth
birthday—which had ever since spirited him back to a world
of high romance whenever he put on the shining helm and
hauberk. Already the qualities of artist, poet, and warrior
were strongly in him, as his father, a prosperous City man,

vaguely noticed when he first took his small eldest son to see the ancient church brasses in the neighbourhood—since he himself had a secret liking for old places. And so they were baleful foes that William was slaying as he slashed off the prickly heads of last year's teasels; his panting pony, older than its master by several years, having slowed now to an ambling walk; and William was content to fall silent for a while and listen to the birds' notes sounding through the forest near by—he could tell the name of every bird by its note alone now—and in front the rooks were already at work, building in the high trees behind his home, Woodford Hall. Then he thought of the other children there, who would only just now be opening sleepy eyes, to see from their high nursery windows the winding course of the Thames, gleaming seven miles southward, set with red-brown sails gliding between cornfields.

The pony turned across a little bridge, and the boy reined in for a minute, as usual, to look down at the long green weeds, that seemed to be weaving an ever-changing pattern as they coiled amid the starry under-water flowers. Then they came to the space of green before the Hall gates; to a place beset with terror to him, because of the ancient stocks and cage standing on it, waiting to catch a victim if they could—the old gravel-stealer and rolling fence maker, so Watts, the footman, told him—or even, if he were not careful about the catching of rabbits *within* his father's park, Master William himself, for being a wee poacher! So he had always, for safety's sake, raced past them as fast as possible, and never slackened till he tumbled off his steed, heart pounding and breathless, in the stable yard; and this particular morning, though he had thought of daring to go by casually, the pony recalled their many previous panics, and changed to a gallop on her own, only stopping within sight of her stable door.

William went upstairs to the airy day-nursery, where breakfast was laid, and his small brothers and sisters already seated in their places. His entry, made with visor down and a great deal of rattling, was greeted with shrill squeals of admiration and terror; but the triumph was brief, for he was seized at once by the under-nurse, his armour firmly removed, led along to be washed and brushed—though his wild black elf-locks were beyond her skill to tame—and finally put into his dull, most unknightly blue pinafore, and sent back to have breakfast.

A few weeks later William was taken by his father to see the church of Minster, in Thanet, and Canterbury Cathedral. Such a wondrous memory had he for all things medieval that, without ever seeing Minster again, as an old man he was able to recall its details from that childhood visit; and as for the cathedral at Canterbury, for weeks after his words flowed in praise of it.

On the morning following his return to Woodford Hall from this visit Emma and Henrietta, the two eldest of his four sisters, not waiting even for their cheese and small ale that were sent up to the nursery at high prime, rushed out after lessons to catch up William, who had already started across the park to the warren. In this favourite retreat a year ago he and Emma had read *The Old English Baron*, and had been so keyed up with excitement that they had returned across the park in a state of utmost dread. But this afternoon the girls were going there to hear all about William's late adventures.

Presently they came to where he lay, fully stretched on the springy turf, and, sitting down beside him, they asked him to begin. So he started to paint for them vivid word pictures of all he had seen on the journey by stagecoach, and at the many little churches his father had stopped to visit on the way. Clearly as in a vision he described the carved and painted beauties in the dim church of Minster (for he seemed to have been born with a love of the Middle Ages, and a knowledge of them, too, that never ceased to astonish his friends). Then he told his sisters about the great cathedral at Canterbury:

its dreamlike wonder of soaring aisles, and far-off flaming windows, and carved and sleeping knights, and, to crown it all, five dizzy minutes gazing down from the battlements of the great tower itself!

" Oh, if only I could build one for myself," he cried, " it should stand away from everything in a great endless corn-field! And I would carve all the pillars and arches and great high windows myself—with stories I've made! About knights in battles and tourneys! Terrible enchantments! Kings and queens! Saints and martyrs! Angels and Demons! Every-where thick with carving and tracery—I know I could do it!" he ended vehemently. And his sisters believed he could too, as they walked back across the park in late sunlight, and entered the white door in the wall of the kitchen garden, all the while his vivid fairy-tale talk flowing on ceaselessly. The air was faintly scented with balm, which grew abundantly under an old blue plum-tree, and they each pinched off some to smell as they passed.

An hour later, his thick black locks smoothed down ready for bed, William was standing at the night-nursery window in his full white nightgown, as he was always allowed to do on summer evenings, while the others were being put to bed ; and now it was the thick, sweet scent of white may-trees on the lawn that he was breathing in so intently, eyes on the farthest sunlit tree-tops, not knowing that scent and memory of these moments would remain lifelong sweet.

By next year William had become too much for his sisters' governess, and soon after his ninth birthday he entered the " Preparatory School for Young Gentlemen," which was kept by the two elderly and prim Misses Arundale at Walthamstow, two miles away. He used to ride there and back daily on his pony, no doubt to the envy of most of the other young gentle-men there.

Whether he was too much for the Misses Arundale or not,

with them he remained until his twelfth year, when Morris, senior, died, and left William as head of the large family. They were well provided for, fortunately, for not long before he died Mr Morris had had an almost miraculous stroke of good luck. Being a bill-broker, he had, in payment of a debt, accepted two hundred and seventy-two pounds' worth of shares in a copper-mine newly opened near Tavistock, and these shares had risen swiftly to the value of something like two hundred thousand pounds! So, besides the arms which the College of Heralds had granted to Mr Morris, with the crest of a white horse's head, which appealed so much to his son's imagination, William inherited an independent income of about nine hundred a year, to come under his absolute control when he should come of age.

Shortly before he died Mr Morris had bought a nomination for William at Marlborough, a public school then newly founded, among the Wiltshire downs, close to Savernake Forest. And so it was that in the winter of 1847-48 William left the kindly Misses Arundale, and the lovely Essex country where he had lived with so few cares and fears, and set out, not without many misgivings, by train and coach for Wiltshire.

Chapter 2

BY COACH TO MARLBOROUGH

"Where goest thou then, O pilgrim, with all these?"
The Hill of Venus

WHAT a melancholy January dusk it was! Not clear, with the primrose sky and early stars that so often bring a dull winter's day to a lovely close, but damp—oh, damp!—and the white fog thick as a blanket, so that nothing beyond the foremost coach-horses could be seen.

And without such weather William had every right to be gloomy, for was not to-morrow to be his first day as new boy at a public school, with three months to get through before he saw his home again? Would his new clothes become more friendly, he wondered, as term wore on, and would he ever get used to wearing this horrible pork-pie cap? Or to having no pony to ride on, and no freedom to go birds-nesting about the woods?

Very grim it seemed, this new life of which he knew so little. If only they had told him what he was to have for supper it might have cheered him, or what kind of room he was to sleep in that night. But he knew nothing—nothing except that he was to be one of a hundred other nameless new boys, going to an unknown life in an unknown place, where there awaited him a heartless system of discipline such as he had never known before.

" One thing I do know," he kept telling himself, " is that no one can order my *mind* about. What ever else happens, my mind is my own, and is free." And from this encouraging thought grew others that comforted him. He remembered the

16

things he had brought with him: the materials for netting, a craft he was good at and loved. His books, above all the great picture-book his father had given him, full of hand-coloured engravings, of castles and cathedrals, and stained-glass windows of fighting angels, and tombs of kings, and knights lying all in their armour just as when they lived. And the present Emma had put into his hand when she said good-bye, packed in its little leather case, with W.M. neatly tooled upon it—a book of curious animals and plants, pictured with quaint woodcuts which showed, as did its print, that it was made quite three hundred years ago!

Why, he would write to Emma to-morrow, and tell her how much he liked it, and all about the new place he was going to; about the country round, the buildings, the other boys, some of whom might even resemble his own brothers! Perhaps he would even be allowed to ask her to send him his silkworms' eggs! Anyhow, he would be able to tell her all about the singing in chapel, the anthems and plainsong which he had heard there were sure to be; and about the books in the school library, which his father had once said would be even larger than the one at Woodford Hall.

"Wake up, young gentleman! You're here now." A rough but kind voice woke him, for he had nodded off to sleep. And, sure enough, "here" they were, for the coach stood, with many other conveyances, near to a brilliantly lit doorway, where countless boys were laughing and greeting one another.

William staggered to his feet and entered with the rest, to where an old clergyman in a bob wig was doing his best to hold a roll-call amid the general hubbub; while from the long tables, laden with pewter-covered dishes, at the farther end of the great dim room, rose the most welcoming scent of steak and onions.

Chapter 3

VISIONS AND HAIL

And they made a lane for us up to the west door; then I put
on my helm and we began to go up the nave, then suddenly the
singing of the monks and all stopped. I heard a clinking and
a buzz of voices in the choir; I turned, and saw that the bright
noon sun was shining on the gold of the priests' vestments, as
they lay on the floor, and on the mail that the priests carried.

So we stopped, and the choir gates swung open, and the
Abbot marched out at the head of *his* men, all fully armed, and
began to strike up the psalm *Exsurgat Deus*.

The Hollow Land

HIS first six months at Marlborough did not much
modify Morris's dislike for school life, with all its intolerable rules, its complete lack of privacy, and its
strong contempt for the tastes of individuals. Luckily his great
physical strength, and still more his furious temper, preserved
him from the bullying which was rife in the boys' schools of
those days—not least at Marlborough, where many a new boy
was swung in a sheet from the top of the main staircase. On
the other hand, he was never what is called popular, and, since
the kindred spirits he found were few, the greater part of his
spare time was spent alone.

The July of '48 was stiflingly hot, so hot that Morris felt
certain that thunder was coming as he sat in the library one
half-holiday, devouring any literature he could find that dealt
with the Middle Ages, which he so loved, and in which he
wished over and over again that he had lived. For the more
he saw of this nineteenth century, the more it seemed to him
soulless and ugly. His energy and strength and furious temper

18

might have served him well had he been a Crusader, but nowadays they were merely useless to him and a nuisance to others. And that other, rarer side of his nature, that inborn delight in beauty, that too he could have satisfied, in those cities and churches and in the unspoilt country of medieval times; while nowadays the growing ugliness of everything that man made, and the way that ugliness seemed steadily to be ruining the beauty of the natural world, exasperated him more and more. He would have found things to do in those days besides fighting: building and carving, or illuminating the lovely painted books, in the colours and patterns of which he felt such inexplicable delight. If only he had been born in Chaucer's day! Life would have been worth living then!

He read till his brain grew tired. At length his fingers grew tired too, of doing nothing but turn over the pages; so he got up and wandered from the library into the schoolroom. To his joy he found he had the great bare room to himself, so he quickly brought out the fishing-net he had been making all the term, and, fastening one end to the master's desk, settled down to work at the other, some yards away. Though his hands looked plump and his fingers were short and square, they moved with a swiftness and skill which would have astonished anyone who could have watched him. Yet he was scarcely conscious that he was working; rather, the fact that his hands were busy freed his mind to meditate as it could not do when he was just sitting still in the library.

His thoughts, of course, were on the coming holidays, with the joyful freedom and leisure that were soon to be his. How he pined for the end of term! He thought he could never endure the last two weeks of it; he must burst somehow with impatience! Impatience with reason, too, for it was during this term that his family had moved from Woodford to a house that promised to be yet more wonderful; for Emma had described it as having a moat, and set in that moat an island, grown with aspen and willow and chestnut. It was at

Walthamstow, and its name was Water House. It was less stately than Woodford, but that was no loss to Morris, who had never been a lover of sophisticated things, but rather of the simplest ones, such as the fishing and bathing and boating that the moat promised, and the little hut which he began to plan to build on the island.

Already he seemed to dip his beloved net into the clear brown water, and, dragging it carefully along, to raise it glittering with the splash and struggle of innumerable fish! Then would come the bonfire, with the blue smoke whirled away through the chestnut boughs; and he would sit to the windward side, holding the sizzling frying-pan, cooking his own quarry for dinner! Oh, how he longed for it! And his own pony to ride on again! To gallop like a knight once more through the meadows, to race through the glades, with all the tiresome world forgotten! Oh, how he *longed* for it all!

Suddenly there was a sharp tap on the window. He looked up, but saw no one. Then came another tap, and another, and then a hundred all at once; and suddenly the view outside became all blurred and grey as the hail swept down, and the thunder roared out, echoing between the hills, and roared again, while the violet lightning flickered, dazzling the sight, so that between its flashes all the world seemed dark.

And all at once the room was loud with voices and hurrying feet on the bare floor. Some one stumbled across his net, but, choking down his temper for once, he quietly put it away, and went to join the others, who stood, many of them dripping, to watch the storm that swept past the windows.

Soon the bell went for chapel, and while the thunder rolled they sang the hundred and fiftieth Psalm—*Laudate Dominum*— till the whole building seemed to quiver. Morris roared his loudest, feeling like some warrior prelate in the days when such music was made. Later the choir sang an anthem, with a duet for two boys' voices, which rose clear as a crystal fountain above the mighty waves of sound which had come before. In the silence of the chapel the voices swept up and down, soaring past one another like swifts in the summer blue; up and down, over and over, till the heart all but stopped beating with the intensity of the beauty. The thunder had rolled away, and as they sang the sun blazed out, so that the dull glass of the west window flashed and glowed suddenly with a brilliance that William never afterwards forgot. And still the voices swept up and down, till his discontent melted away, turning to such absolute delight in the loveliness that he felt almost as if his longed-for Middle Ages were come back at last.

Chapter 4

MONOLITHS

Birdalone said: " Tell me now of the tales that be told of that valley." Quoth Leonard: " They be many; but the main of them is this: that those Greywethers be giants of yore agone."
The Water of the Wondrous Isles

WILLIAM and Vere had been looking forward eagerly for the last week to this particular day, for it was one of their rare *whole* holidays, and they had planned to use it to the best advantage in an expedition to Avebury and Silbury Hill.[1] Vere Beauclere had already heard all about these places from his friend, for William had lately visited them on his own, and come back and read up all he could find about the Druidical circles and prehistoric barrows that give to the quiet Wiltshire downs a quality of utter mystery, a sense of indescribable awe and sadness.

Here was the day, then, and they had planned to start out at nine o'clock. But well before that hour had struck from St Peter's tower they were away, mounting the slopes northward, without a glance back at the dog-eared belfry or the roofs of Marlborough town. " Let's be at the top before it strikes!" cried Morris, his cheeks glowing from the hurry they had had to get away before the rest of the school dispersed through the surrounding country, and added, perhaps, to the perfect company of two.

They began to run, the mild downland wind strengthening against them as they faced it, their bottles of small ale clinking together merrily in Morris's home-made scrip, and making

[1] Ancient British stone-circle and barrow.

22

them both laugh breathlessly at the thought of how they had cornered old Hopsack, the second steward, and plied him with silver coins, and silver words, until he could resist no more, and smuggled into their bag a small banquet.

They gained the top, and turned to look back down at the way they had come. The pinnacles of St Peter's were all that showed now of the town in the valley, and as their gaze wandered away to where Savernake Forest piled itself deeply over the farther slopes, and the higher sweep of Martinsell Hill lay blue upon the skyline, the sound of a bell came faintly up to them.

" There! It's striking! We've raced it by quite two minutes!" exclaimed little Beauclere, his small chest still heaving. (It was always a strain to keep up with William Morris, in every way, but perhaps mostly in the way he hurled himself along towards any object that had captivated his imagination; and he had the added advantage of being very strong and energetic, in appearance older by several years than Vere, though there was scarcely a year between them.)

Their way lay across open downland now, over which wound a faint grass track, probably traced out three thousand years ago by the first downland dwellers, Morris supposed— though why couldn't they walk straight, he added, laughing. Yet to the track they kept, since the rougher grass on either side was heavily hung with moisture, for a sudden storm had swept over the country as they sat at breakfast, making them momentarily desperate with impending disappointment. Yet now, in the fresh, sparkling sunlight, the lonely hawthorn⁄trees growing here and there about the downs flashed white as new⁄fallen snow. To the west the sky was piled with huge white clouds, *so* bright, *so* enormous, towering up bank on bank, that Morris drew deep breaths of delight as he gazed at the topmost edges, almost over their heads.

" If you look at them and breathe your deepest you seem to draw their strength into you. Try it, Vere!" said William encouragingly. Vere obeyed, trying hard to feel the stronger for it, and perhaps he did; for all at once great heavy drops began to fall on their faces, faster and faster, and they started to run towards the nearest thorn-trees, and presently both boys tumbled together beneath the shelter of leaning snowy boughs.

The tangle of thorny twigs, thick with flowers though they were, gave little shelter from the sheeting rain which now veiled downs and sky. So they crept farther in, and made a tent of their dark green ulsters, and when they were settled Vere said, " Now tell me some more of the story you've made up, about the knights of the Castle Terrible, and Peerless Gard, and the princess who was shut up in a tower in the sea— you didn't finish that story, you know."

William hesitated. " Do you mind if I don't just now? I can't think of anything but those strange places we are going to see—I wonder and wonder however those little brown early Britons, with their rough implements and dark minds, could have raised a ring of such ponderous stones, and piled up a perfectly round hill as high as a church spire. I would like to think and think about it, until I *saw* them working on them, as I can see the medieval people living and building and painting when I think of *them*. Oh, dear! *How* I wish I had been a monk in the thirteenth century! Or a master weaver of storied tapestry, or a builder of ships, or a carver when they made cathedrals like the one I saw at Canterbury!"

Vere listened in silence. He found it hard to think of an answer to William when he talked like this; his own words sounded so silly after such learned ones, and spoilt, too, the pictures William made in one's mind when he spoke.

The sky above was blue again now, as they could see through the black branches and white flowers over their heads, so they left their shelter for the grassy track again. The sun too came out with dazzling brilliance as the cloud-banks sped away over the woods of Martinsell, swiftly as they had come.

Presently the track led downward, and they entered an

empty vale, which seemed the lonelier for the great grey boulders with which it was strewn. As often in valleys, the lack of freshness in the air gave them both an irresistible inclination to rest, and they sat down together on one of the smooth stones which were already drying fast in the sun.

At the sound of their voices a hare leapt up from his form some way down the valley, and bounded up the turfy slope.

"Sapper would have liked a shot at that; he's always talking about the shoots he goes on with his father in the holidays. Their place is full of antlers, and stuffed animals his family have killed, he says. I *can't* see how people enjoy hurting and killing—as some of the fellows do here—can you?"

"Yes," said William definitely, "I've thought it out. It's because they want to be greater than something or some one. And they haven't a particular cleverness of their own—or they're too lazy to find out what it is. So they make themselves winners or tyrants the easiest way: by taking on some one much weaker than them. Like that beastly business of sheeting all the new boys till they buy themselves free, and trapping and squalling [1] the wild things in the forest."

"I wish I had a cleverness," sighed Vere wistfully, admiring his friend's sturdy shape and determined profile.

"You *have*!" cried William, turning and thumping his shoulder affectionately. "As long as you want to know about things, and think and puzzle about them on your own, and always want to know more and more and more—you're *bound* to have a cleverness in the end! And one of the most worth having."

"It's very nice of you to cheer me up, saying that. And I shall certainly try to make the wonderings grow into something useful. You seem to have *several* clevernesses, though—netting, and story-making, and scribbling, and *knowing*—that most of all! I *wonder* what you will do that is clever when you grow up!"

[1] Killing animals by throwing a stick weighted with lead.

"I can't say at all yet," said William ; "perhaps because I've not tried hard enough at any one thing yet. But I don't like doing only one thing, that's the trouble. I want to be able to do many, *many* things—all the things that can be done with one's hands—I don't mean just thinking work."

Each thought his own thoughts for a while. The pale, round stones scattered all down the shallow valley set William's mind weaving tales of enchantments about their origin. A laugh from Vere called him back.

"I was thinking of old Sourface and Treacle Bolley [1]! He's sure to be teased out of his floury wits to-day by Upper School, after the last fury call he made on the Master. They'd kill him if they dared, I believe, for sneaking."

"Poor Treacle Bolley—always being told to 'git up' with that lazy old sack of flour on his back! I'm sorry enough for the creature, what with miller and baiters." William smothered a yawn, wondering why he was feeling more and more drowsy.

"Do you feel you could go straight to sleep, Vere?"

"I've been feeling that for some time!" Vere replied, with a yawn that set William yawning too, until they laughed at each other and jumped up.

"Come on," said William firmly, "there's something strange about this valley! We shall probably go to sleep for a hundred years if we don't get out quickly!" and, taking Vere's hand, he ran up the slope, and soon the downland wind was blowing in their faces again.

How fresh and beautiful it was on that grassy upland over which the larks were singing! The wind raced past them, silvering the grass, which was so wondrously green after the shower. The only trees were the clumps of age-old beeches, in one of which a whole flock of pigeons was cooing, but sped away at their approach. The two boys watched them till they vanished somewhere over the distant woods which showed beyond the Kennet valley, far away southward.

[1] A local miller and his donkey.

Presently their track crossed another one, running from east to west straight as the crow flies, and known as the Ridgeway, and not long afterwards they came into the first fields of Avebury itself. On a little farther, and then, there before them, only a brief stretch of pasture away, were the great pale stones, showing between thinly leaved beech⁄boles. Across this last field the two boys ran, careless of the wet grass now—and in a minute or two their downland path had led them right into the middle of the great circle, and they were standing beneath the nearest towering monolith.

" How quiet they are! " whispered Vere presently. " Almost as if they were listening or waiting for something! "

" Perhaps they are," answered William. " This is where the Druids—they were the high priests of the ancient Britons—this is where they made their sacrifices to the sun and the seasons, and held strange and terrible rites for the sake of the welfare of the people. They wore white robes, and flowing silver beards, and long hair bound with oak⁄leaves. Think how fearful the sight must have been when they prayed at this altar to the moon! But don't you find it hard to believe that such things *have* ever happened here, where the sunlight gleams so kindly on the stones, and deep grasses grow against them, with such a lovely sky above? "

" We could sit down on this flat stone and have our lunch here—if you'd like to, that is," suggested Vere hopefully.

And William immediately realized that he was very hungry too. The scrip was unpacked, and bottles set up in the shade of the stone, and they both turned their thoughts to the enjoy⁄ment of old Hopsack's cold venison pie, pickled onions, and new milk⁄loaves.

The sun shone through to where they rested, hot now as in June, dappling the ground with leaf shadows. William let his mind roam back to the dapple⁄shadowed glades of hornbeam that had enclosed his earliest memories—his first story⁄world. Then he thought of Water House, and all the magic that a moat and island had added to his life, and at once started to ache for the holidays, still over two months away. He would seek consolation in a long letter to Emma, all about the expedition and other pleasant things. Cheered by this thought, he finished his ale, and after walking once more round the great ring of upright stones they turned southward to Silbury Hill.

It was full afternoon now; the great banks of cloud had drawn away to the western horizon, and the sky was clear except for a few soft white islands left behind. They saw the hill before them, its outline showing clearly against the silver country beyond.

" We'll come to the water-meadow presently," said William, after they had been walking along silently for a while. " I hope they haven't let the dykes fill up since I last came here! But we'll get to the hill somehow even if they have—I *must* stand on the top once more! "

The water-meadow had not been flooded, however, and they managed to reach the base of the great mound without getting wet.

The ascent was made, with much puffing and panting, and there they stood at last, higher up than the cross on the church spire, as William had said, with all the country round, as far as eye could see, seeming to ebb away from the acclivity to nothing and then sky. They lay down on their backs and stared up at the dome of blue above them. Suddenly William sat up.

" Do you love being alive, Vere? " he asked; and as the other boy was wondering what he meant he continued: " Sometimes—up here, for instance, or when I'm in the forest on specially perfect days—sometimes, even, for just a moment on quite ordinary days in school, I feel a bursting happiness in everything! But always, directly afterwards, I feel as if all the joy had slipped from me, and I want to go and look for it, though I don't know where. Netting helps, but it doesn't seem enough. I think building something, a church or a roof-tree hall, would make me happy all the time the work lasted—and it could last a long time if one set about decorating every inch of the place with paintings and carvings of every leaf and flower and animal—as they used to! It must have been glorious to have such things to make for one's daily work!"

Vere longed to be able to say that he too had felt just the same, that nothing seemed to him lovelier than the lives of those calm monk-historians William had told him about—but there was little use in longing for such a life, since his father had determined upon the Army as a career for him.

William rose now, and, picking up one of the many little white snail-shells that lay about the almost turfless ground, said it must be time for them to start back to school. So they slipped down the steep hillside to the water-meadow again. Turning away from the sun, they walked for a mile or so along the Ridgeway that they had crossed earlier in the day, until it died away into plain grassland near a lane leading to the village of Fifield. William could not resist delaying for a moment to go and look at Fifield church, hidden low down among protecting trees; then on they went schoolward without delay, and were just in time not to have to arrive breathless for evening service.

What a lovely day it had been! All through the droning of the prayers William could not keep his mind from thinking how he would presently be telling Emma all about it.

Chapter 5

"STINGBOTTOM'S DOWN!"

The grim king fumes at the council board:
" Three more days, and then the sword;

Three more days, and my sword through his head;
Above his white brows, pale and dead."

Therefore though it be long ere day,
Take axe and pick and spade, I pray.

Break down the dams all over the plain:
God send us three more days such rain:

Block all the upland roads with trees;
The little Tower with no great ease

Is won, I warrant; bid them bring
Much sheep and oxen, everything

That spits are wont to turn with; wine
And wheaten bread, that we may dine

In plenty each day of the siege;
Good friends, ye know me no hard liege.

The Little Tower

THE rich fragrance of Latakia filled the masters' commonroom as Dr Suger puffed importantly at his great church-
warden, seeking for words in which to address the
anxious group of younger men, who seemed to be expecting
him, by some magic of his own, to save the day.

Since Guy Fawkes night the situation had sped from bad to worse, and worse still. The celebrations in court that night had been dangerously riotous; nor were the disciplinary measures taken by the Master—the expulsion of the most popular ringleaders and the gating of the whole rest of the school—such as a wise man would have taken; for it only stung the unruly spirits into greater unruliness, while those who had hitherto been tractable were transformed by the gating into rebels, heart and soul. And last night the gates had been broken and Peviar, the porter, savaged, in a riot so alarming that poor Dr Suger, who had been in Paris during the Terror as a boy, felt that Marlborough was fast becoming little less dangerous!

" Certainly we must take the bull by the horns," Suger said, " but the question is, how? The Master's penalty—an hour's penal drill before breakfast and yet stricter bounds—will be as useless as it is mistaken; and as for what will follow— remember my words, gentlemen—I tell you plainly it won't fall short of mutiny! "

The younger men glanced uneasily at one another. How could they, a handful of fifteen patient scholars, face a mutiny of over five hundred tough and lively boys, already beyond control, and now stung into fury by the Master's ill-advised attempt at punishing the offenders?

" Why, only last week, gentlemen, as you know, my col- league Gray's wig was set ablaze as he dozed for a moment in his divinity class! Last Tuesday, as you know, in Dr Soutar's Latin class a bonfire was kindled, and a swarm of rats, mice, and birds let out! Such happenings mean the end, my friends —the end! "

" Well," broke in Mr Wood, the mathematics master (" Stingbottom," as he was called), " I'm damned if I'll sit still under it. Give it them hot, I say, red-hot! I've had enough of spare the rod! " His eyes flashed and his whiskers bristled, as he straddled before the fire, his hands clasped behind him beneath his gown, flicking his calves ceaselessly with the long, supple cane whose use had earned him his name. To a casual observer his appearance might have suggested a steel pistonrod; by those who knew him better he was known as a malicious busybody, a spiteful old feline who was oddly oldwomanish in his grumbles and waspish temper.

"Your remarks about the rod are wise, Stingbottom," Suger agreed, " but things here have been more mistaken still : when it should have been spared it has been used, and when used spared. In that way, gentlemen, revolutions are caused. When I was in Paris in ninetytwo . . ."

The bell interrupted him, and the company uneasily dispersed, each wondering what the morrow would bring.

Nor were their fears vain, for next morning, which opened with driving snow, no one came in answer to the summons to the general penal drill. The snow drove faster, whirling past the great yewtrees before the Mansion, piling high on the windowsills, and dropping down the chimney with intermittent hisses into the commonroom fire. To those who were gathered there the hisses sounded full of angry import, for one after another had come in with the news that no boys had come to his first morning class. At last the whole staff was there, and last of all the Master, no longer a gentle and urbane scholar, but gazing from face to face like a lost child.

Meanwhile in Morris's dormitory preparations for a siege were going on with medieval thoroughness. Doors and corridors were barricaded with cupboards, boxes, tables, beds —everything movable. Stores, smuggled in during the last week, were being opened for breakfast; while everything that could be used as a missile lay piled ready to hand near the windows.

But no sign of attack came till dusk, when, after a cheerless supper of sweets, apples, and cake, the captain of the dormitory thought fit to harangue his men. As he began, the first blows of the assaulters sounded on the doors below. Then, with cheers, roars, and squeals, and shouts of " Liberty ! " " To hell with Stingbottom ! " " Down with the Master ! " the defenders leapt to their posts at the windows, and, leaning out into the driving snow, poured a volley of stones, sticks, books, and basins of water on to the enemy below.

" Hurrah, Stingbottom's down ! " shouted some one presently, and all crowded to see where Mr Wood, who had led the assault on the door with a woodcutter's axe in place of his cane, sprawled dazed, kicking and cursing, deluged with a pailful of some noisome liquid showered on him from above. His discomfiture, though, was short, and stung him into greater rage, and soon his axe was crashing on the door with a thunder that chilled to the vitals the more timid among the defenders. But Morris's spirit was aflame as he roared, " Come on, you fellows ! Sally, I tell you—sally ! Come on ! Follow me to the barricades ! Hurrah for freedom ! " Whirling a heavy poker, with a broad wooden bog-lid for a shield, Morris rushed towards the stairs, his eyes blazing, and locks bristling with the thrill of battle. But he and those who followed him were recalled as soon by a greater danger—that of the ladder-tops that were being thrown up to the windows— and the fight began in earnest, the stout defenders grappling with yet stouter college servants and labourers from the estate. For some time all seemed lost, till darkness and a still sharper blizzard came to the rescue, and the attack was called off for the night. The besieged spent it with unbroken hearts, but with teeth chattering with the cold, for all bedding had been hurled with the mattresses from the windows. Far into the night plans of campaign were discussed, and day dawned on grim determination and unbowed spirits.

The fighting, though, was over, for presently a truce was called, and a general amnesty declared. The rebels were asked to state their grievances, and before very long things were going smoothly enough. It was not till some years later, however, when the absurdly small staff was enlarged and Dr Cotton from Rugby became Master, that Marlborough began to acquire tradition, and to be known as the great public school that it is to-day.

As for Morris, though he shared in the Revolt like every one else, those of the staff who had behaved kindly towards him, especially his housemaster, were by no means forgotten. Richardson, a master of Morris's time, told how at the end of a term a small boy came to his housemaster holding something behind him, saying that he wanted to say good-bye, and, as the housemaster had been so good to him sometimes when he was not feeling too happy, he wished to make him a parting present. He then produced from behind his back a beautifully carved walking-stick, made of Forest wood. The house-master told Richardson that it was so beautifully done that in thanking the boy he told him that if he had not settled his career he should be a wood-carver. The boy's name was William Morris.

Chapter 6

DEVONSHIRE CREAM

Oh! to hear that *tchink* again! I felt the notch my sword made
in his, and swung out at him; but he guarded it and returned
on me; I guarded right and left, and grew warm, and opened
my mouth to shout, but knew not what to say; and our sword
points fell on the floor together: then when we had panted
awhile, I wiped from my face the blood that had been dashed
over it, shook my sword and cut at him, then we spun round
and round in a mad waltz to the measured music of our meeting swords, and sometimes either wounded the other somewhat,
but not much, till I beat down his sword onto his head, that
he fell grovelling, but not cut through. Verily, therefore, my lips
opened mightily with " Mary rings!"

The Hollow Land

AFTER the tumult at Marlborough that winter, William's
mother thought it better that he should work under a
private tutor until he was ready to go up to Oxford.
For this purpose a kindly young clergyman-schoolmaster was
chosen—the Rev. F. B. Guy—who took a few pupils in his
house at Walthamstow. Here William made such progress
in classics that he was well in advance of his age when he
took his matriculation examination at Oxford, and he passed
without difficulty.

The last summer before he entered college he went with
Mr Guy and some other students to a farm in Devonshire,
and great was his delight when he found that the farm was a
delapidated manor house of the fourteenth century, with stone
walls like those of a castle, and a great stone-flagged hall,
furnished with a splendid refectory table, at which they were
to work and feast.

.　　　.　　　.　　　.　　　.　　　.

"There's them young gentlemen at it again! A⁄brawling and a⁄howling, and squealing out demon⁄like; you'd think 'twas Tregeagle hisself was in the parlour!" Poor Mrs Trelawney's hands shook as she prepared to carry in the monstrous tea which study of the classics, with singlestick, bathing, bear⁄fights, and the air of North Devon made always welcome to the reading⁄party who were staying on Trelawney's farm. And at singlestick they certainly were. Even Mr Guy, who had known William since childhood, felt a little alarmed as his opponent, driven by a pitiless rain of blows, staggered backward over a sofa and lay apparently senseless on the floor, while William only looked round calmly, evidently expecting some one else to take him on. "Here is tea," said Mr Guy firmly. "Morris, go and wash. Singlestick is over for to⁄day."

Oh, what a tea it was! Only those of you who know North Devon will know quite what it was like, while those who don't will scarcely believe me if I tell them. For, besides the new farmhouse bread which Morris so loved, and the clotted cream and honey and several kinds of jam with which it was to be loaded; besides the seed⁄cake and heavy fruit⁄cake, brandy⁄flavoured and sticky; besides the radishes, water⁄cress, and big pink prawns, the table bore a broad cherry⁄tart, and a splendid ham for the especially hungry.

And didn't they do justice to it! Best of all the quiet philosopher, with the sandy hair and little, sleepy eyes, that gleamed now and then with such generous fire! And next to him the thin and seemingly starved young inquisitor, who always wore black, and spectacles so thick that you never saw quite what his eyes were like! And next to him William himself! Even Mr Guy, tired with forcing Demosthenes into unwilling heads, and with the never⁄ceasing anxiety of being the shepherd of such a flock, even *his* eyes sparkled at the sight of the pale pink cherries, shining from their deep and crisp yet tender couch of freshly risen pastry.

William ate and drank largely but silently. His longing to be a warrior of old time had almost seemed accomplished, until his opponent's fall and the arrival of tea had brought him back to the dull, adventureless world into which he seemed to have been born by some mistake. Not that he liked the cruelty of fighting (his opponent's bleeding and bruised appearance shocked him and stung his conscience); but the freedom of an age, of past or future, when men of energy had something to do! Something better than fighting, better than building even—something truly worth giving one's life to!

What it was he did not know, nor was to know till years afterwards. Meanwhile he felt only that he had some great, some exceptional power within him, and not to know where or how to use it made him feel strangely restless and disappointed. So he did his best to dismiss the feeling, and to join the others in their talk of this thing and that.

They talked of Oxford, and of Exeter, the college where William was to go next January. He had matriculated last June, and should have gone up in October, but the college was so full that he had been put off for a term. Mr Guy spoke vividly of the almost medieval grey-walled city, of the lovely country round, and of the splendid freedom and fullness of undergraduate life, until William began to look forward to January more than he could say.

They talked of the Church, and of the many differences there were at that time between prominent men in the Church of England; of the effects of the Oxford Movement, and of the way the Catholics had gained ground in England steadily since Newman's conversion, seven years previously, until, just two years ago, Catholic bishops had been installed all over the country, to the intensest indignation of staunch Protestants. This very summer Newman was on trial for his attack on Dr Achilli, the chief exponent of Protestant opinion, and no one knew how the trial would end.

But though William had chosen, or had let others choose

for him, the Church as a profession, he felt little in common with the other Church students he knew. They discussed ritual, vestments, incense, and the worship of the Virgin Mary, and Mr Guy told them how churchmen were divided for and against such things. William ardently defended them, as being some of the last surviving beauties of the medieval life that he so loved. But he found that his arguments carried little or no weight with the others, who all seemed to look at things from one point of view only—a moral one. And when he pressed his point again, Mr Guy's remark, " Morris, you should be an artist, not a pastor of souls," though truer than either of them knew, only made William angrier, because of the unspoken feeling in his heart that both were the same thing.

Chapter 7

NED JONES

Queen Mary's crown was gold,
King Joseph's crown was red,
But Jesus' crown was diamond
That lit up all the bed
Mariæ Virginis

Ships sail through the heaven
With red banners dress'd,
Carrying the planets seven
To see the white breast
Mariæ Virginis
Carol in *The Hollow Land*

THE stars were shining brilliantly past the pinnacles of
St Mary's, Oxford, and very silent and awe-inspiring
seemed the frost-bound world to the thin figure, with
the soft pale hair and anxious eyes, who was walking up
Magpie Lane from his lodgings to his first dinner in Hall.
Edward Burne Jones—for that was his name—was cold already, for no fire had been laid to greet him in his tiny room
with the sloping ceiling, where he was to work till there was
room for him in college; and as he turned from the Turl into
Exeter, and fell in with the stream of other men going into
Hall, none of whom he knew, but all of whom seemed to
know one another, he began to feel almost miserable.

Yet somehow the entrance to Hall was accomplished; he
was shown to the Freshmen's table, where some one pressed a
tankard of "xxxxx" upon him, and soon he found himself looking round with fingers and toes pleasantly tingling

39

back to life, and feeling that Oxford was a not unfriendly place after all.

Not till now had he dared look up, but directly he did so he recognized the donor of the "xxxxx," which brought him out of his dream; for who was it but his next-door neighbour of the examination last June, whose appearance had excited his admiration and curiosity—his thick black mane, his fine, strong yet sensitive face, and his eyes that looked with such trusting frankness, such thoughtful seriousness, on to the world. He had had no chance to speak to him then; but his name he knew, for when the examination was over he had seen him fold his paper and write on it "William Morris."

"Hullo, Morris," he said; "so you got through the exam too."

" My wig, of course; it was child's-play. But I'm glad you did too. I wanted to talk to you then. You look like a human being, you know; and I believe they're rare in Oxford. Have some more ' Five X.'"

" No, thank you; I've not finished this yet. But it's good on a freezing night."

" Cold, is it? Well, I suppose it is. But Oxford looks fine under snow. Where do you live?"

"In Magpie Lane. It's only a garret, and the old thing hasn't given me a fire."

" Oh, near Merton tower; you're lucky. I'm in Oriel Street. What about coming round after dinner? I've got a huge fire."

And not long after, dinner over, they were in the snow again, as if the fire and candle-lit hall had been a dream. Round the corner they went, where the rising wind whistled between the high, dark walls of Brasenose Lane, blowing the powdery snow into their faces, and flapping their thin gowns about them. But, oh, what beauty, when they came out into the great square behind St Mary's! For the moon had risen past All Souls towers and the forest of lesser pinnacles around them, and all was scintillating in its dazzling light.

The towers had been silent till then, but now the air seemed full of the clanging of bells. They looked up in silence at the Bodleian, rising like a cliff, with its crown of fine tracery, and its many windows sparkling in the moon and starlight; up at the towering mountain of the Radcliffe Camera, to its leaded cupola, past which some tiny clouds were drifting; up to St Mary's, the finest, William thought, of all the spires he had ever seen, its carven bishops and kings showing clearly, and its weathercock a-gleam, facing the bitter wind from the north.

"What do you think of all this?" he asked his companion.

"It's like a vision of the Middle Ages," was the answer; "but better than a vision. It's life as I always hoped it would be."

Morris had truly a splendid fire, as they saw even beneath his door, as they groped their way up the steep and pitch-dark stair. They sat for some time basking in the firelight, which lit the room so brilliantly that Morris did not light the candles. Then, when they had thawed, he brought out from the mahogany sideboard decanters and glasses; and from other well-stocked cupboards tobacco and a new meerschaum for himself, and cheroots for the visitor. And soon the conversation lost its first shyness and formality, and became as one between friends who have come together after a long parting, and cannot find words to express all they have to say to each other!

For this was the first time that either of them had ever met a man like himself, though both were nearly twenty. And glad indeed they must have been! They seemed to discuss everything under the sun as they sat there in the firelight, with the frost-bound world shut out so well by the heavy curtains and shutters, all but the tolling of the great bell from Tom Tower at Christ Church, which came to them down the chimney, where the great logs were blazing.

Each found his likes and dislikes, his interests, his values of the world in which he found himself echoed in the other. And this, strangely enough, though their pre-Oxford lives had been as different as possible. For the pale-haired youth had been as poor as Morris was rich; and was an only child, with no mother. He had grown up in Birmingham, in a house in a street, and had been a boy at King Edward's School there. Perhaps, had not both chosen the Church as a calling—a choice in which both proved later to have been mistaken—neither would have come to Oxford. Such was the chance that brought these lifelong friends together.

Apart from Jones, Morris found few other close friends at Pembroke, and none at Exeter. They consorted chiefly with a small group of Pembroke men who had been schoolfellows of Jones's, and shared his and Morris's tastes.

As for the ' learning' of Oxford, as expounded by the dons, it was certainly dry and uninspiring enough, and to the two friends, who, as time went on, realized more and more that their intellects were creative rather than academic, it could make little appeal. And, although Morris learnt to read Greek and Latin literature with ease, he could never bring himself to take the least interest in grammatical construction; while, as for spelling, he refused to be bound by arbitrary rules, even in his own language (and quite possibly he was right, for hard-and-fast rules in spelling there were none before about 1700).

Thus the wide knowledge which he and Jones acquired at Oxford was gained chiefly through independent reading, for they read and discussed together till the small hours, night after night. Indeed, as with many another distinguished man, the great value of Oxford life to both lay in the leisure and freedom to develop each in his individual way that this life gave them: this and the lifelong inspiration of the beauty of that yet unspoilt and almost medieval city, and of the wondrous wooded hills and fair river plains among which it lay.

Chapter 8

THE BARD

" The red wine
Under the roadside bush was clear; the flies,
The dragon flies I mind me most, did shine
In brighter arms than ever I put on. . . .

" And so we entered Verveille wood next day,
In the afternoon; through it the highway runs,
Twixt copses of green hazel, very thick,
And underneath, with glimmering of suns,
The primroses are happy; the dews lick
The soft green moss. . . ."

Early Romances

DIRECTLY after breakfast one spring morning of '54
Morris stuffed a piece of paper into his pocket and
hurried along to Ted's [1] rooms, which were close to his,
for both were living in college now. But he found them

[1] Edward Burne Jones is hereafter referred to as Ted and Ned inter-
changeably.

empty, the bedroom door left wide, and stood uncertainly considering for a moment. Ted would probably be in chapel, calmly murmuring on his knees, unconscious of the need for his ears elsewhere. The only thing was to wait till he came back, and try not to fidget too much with his things, left so tidily arranged. Morris went up and sat on the narrow window-seat, leaning his head back against the frame to gaze out at the space of April blue above. It seemed aching for the young leaves to lie against it; their delicate lines and shadows would make the blue so much more precious where it showed through. He *must* see them against it like that as soon as possible, while the knight's death was still vivid in his thoughts. Ted must come away to the river to-day.

These thoughts were broken presently by the sound of foot-steps on the staircase, and Morris jumped to his feet with a shout of pleasure as Jones came in.

"Hullo, Top!" ("Topsy" was the name given to Morris by his friends on account of his thick black mane.) "I was just deciding to come and find you." Morris pushed him towards an armchair, and sat down astride a trafalgar opposite.

"Ted, I can't wait a moment. I never could keep sur-prises. It isn't much of a one, and I'm not really at all proud of it; but it's the first one I've made, you see, so I was rather pleased about it, and wanted you to hear it as soon as it was done; but that was late last night after you left, so I came round here with it this morning."

Ted cut in as Morris stopped for breath. "But what *is* it? For heaven's sake tell me! What ever is it you've made?"

Morris drew the piece of paper from his pocket.

"It's a poem, I think," he said.

Ted jumped up at once to take it, but his friend pushed him back. "No, I'll read it to you," he said, and, putting his arms round the chair-back, he tilted it back and forth continuously as he read in a chanting voice:

44

"THE WILLOW AND THE RED CLIFF

"Elaine, Elaine, seen at last,
Where the river runneth past
The Red Cliff, and shades are cast

"O'er my face as I look up.
Stoop to me your mouth's curved cup,
Ere I faint with looking up

"To your face through willow leaves.
Golden hair like lowland sheaves;
Sad eyes that the clear light grieves;

"Sad lips leaning down to me;
Long hands that I scarce can see
For the flowers they hold for me.

"I would move but cannot lift
Helm or hand for this great rift
In my side. The waters drift

"Us apart. I called thy name
When his sword came like a flame.
I fell for you without blame.

"Red Cliff makes your face full pale.
Speak once ere the late light fail.
She has loosed the cord to trail

"Out through water flowers gold.
To his words no words she told.
To his eyes her eyes were cold.

"Then she let the flowers fall slow
On his cast back helm and brow,
Down through willow wands leant low.

"Till the waters took the skiff
From her memory and her life,
From the Willow and Red Cliff."

As he ceased and looked up, Ted's eyes were resting on him
with such an expression of wonder and admiration that he
had to laugh at being taken so seriously. But Ted refused to

take it lightly. The images and rhymes of the poem had
startled in him new, strange feelings. He was trying in his
mind to capture their significance, also to realize the importance of this moment—for all at once Topsy had become a
man of genius!

"I can only say I think it's *wonderful*! Topsy, what *has*
happened to you? In one night you've become a poet of the
first order! Is it really the first you've written? One can
scarcely believe it—it sounds so skilled—the rhymes all going
so beautifully, and the metre, like music—*and* the *place* you
take one to! So clear, I feel I've been there really—and seen
her looking down on *me*—oh, Topsy, you are a strangely
wonderful fellow!"

Morris was surprised at this reception of his poem. It had
certainly pleased him to discover he could actually write one;
but it had been so easy, he felt there could not really be much
of value in it.

"Well, I'm very glad you like it, Ted. Perhaps I shall
write some more, now I have started. If so, and if you can
bear to listen, I shall always read them to you. Now, I thought,
if you were willing, it would be lovely to get away from our
rooms to-day, and walk over to Wytham woods, by Binsey.
The meadows will be perfect, and we can talk—oh, about so
many pleasant things—at least, I feel I could!"

"So could I, Top! Away with dull learning! Let's go
at once, before I find I have a tutorial with old Greyface!
As he's always asleep when I arrive he'll never miss me!"

A quarter of an hour later they were able to look back at the
many spires and towers of Oxford from the wide expanse of
Port Meadow. Away to the right, as far as eye could see, the
vast plain lay smoothly green, scattered with grazing cattle
and horses. The river winding to the west of it had sunk
back within its banks since February's floods, and could now
be discerned only by solitary sails tacking upstream on the
fresh east wind. The two young men breathed it in gladly, as

they reached a bridge poised high over a glassy weir, and saw the wind whipping the wavelets back. For a short distance their way lay among crumbling river banks, and Morris waited while Ted descended among the reeds to find and draw a tall spray of wild forget-me-not flowers. Then they turned down to the left across a marshy mead, crossed by stepping-stones, leading to a group of low-roofed cottages and a small, whitewashed inn in a narrow garden.

" Let's stop at the Perch and drink a bottle of red wine— they have fine old Stilton, too, as a rule," suggested Morris, as they neared the tiny village of Binsey.

The air inside the dark, low-ceilinged parlour was conscious with hoary ancients, so they carried their bottle and cheese out to a seat in the garden. Vivid glimpses of green meadows and flashing water, the smacking of a sail as it turned, came to them distantly through high whitethorn hedges.

After this interlude they went on across several deep meadows, up a ploughed field, and at last into the woods that had risen so blue before them at the beginning of their walk. Here was perfect spring-time. A stream-like murmur of birds' voices filled the wood, and somewhere a hidden stream itself was falling. From distant higher depths faintly the cuckoo sounded, and all about among the trees wild daffodils were growing.

While Jones made drawings of flowers and trees, Morris lay on his back, gazing up at the leaves and sky, seeing all just as he had longed to do.

In the late afternoon they ascended a meadow above the woods, and, resting on the barkless boughs of a fallen elm, worn smooth and silver by many winters, looked down over the tree-tops at river and plain and spires, and, beyond, the blue heights of Shotover.

They began to discuss Ruskin, whose *Stones of Venice* had appeared not long ago, and which both were reading eagerly. To Morris, especially, Ruskin seemed a wonderful guiding light, and the only writer on art who had come near the truth as to why modern taste was so deplorable.

"He's a genius, Ned," he affirmed. "Everything he says is so utterly true. All the things you half knew before he makes clear—and, oh, the language he writes in! Such imagery! I've never seen anything like it!"

"Nor have I. But tell me about the last chapter, which you've read and I haven't. Didn't you say it was something extraordinary?"

"Yes. *The Nature of Gothic* it's called; not that what he says about Gothic is so important, but he does say something about nowadays which I've never heard said before; yet I've always felt it, or something like it. He tells you why mass-produced things are so hideous and hand-made things so beautiful. He compares the making of modern glass to the making of old Venetian. One is done mechanically, by some one who sits tending a machine all day, with never a chance to show his individuality in any way, or take any joy in his work, so the result is quite soulless; while the man who made the Venetian glasses did each one by hand, expressing his fancy as he wished, like an artist painting a picture. And, though his glass may not be so clear as the machine-made tumbler, yet it is more beautiful by far, because the maker put his own soul into it, and his pleasure in making it is imprinted on it. In fact, that's what the beauty is—it's the expression of the enjoyment he felt in the making of it.

"And the same with Gothic carving, as opposed to Roman. For Roman were done by slaves, measured to a design, while the carvings on Gothic cathedrals were done by free men, each of whom was allowed to express his fancy in the flowers and figures he carved; which is why Gothic capitals are so varied and beautiful and Roman ones so dull, even though they may be better smoothed and finished—yet quite soulless."

"I see what you mean, Top. Why didn't we think of it

before! So that's why we like Gothic so much! We always did, yet could never say why!"

"Yes, and that's why factory-made things are so ugly—they bear the stamp of joyless toil; so, however well they're finished, the essential beauty's lacking. He tells you never to value finish for its own sake, but to forgive all roughness if only you can see that the maker enjoyed what he did—for then it's beautiful, however rough. Why, how true it is! Why *didn't* we think of it, Ned!"

"Never mind, Top; you think of many things just as good, you know. But he's a great man, all the same."

Returning home in the twilight, they were nearing St Giles', when a gentleman hurrying in the opposite way passed close to them, and Jones, who was nearest him, suddenly caught Topsy's arm.

"It's *him*!" he said breathlessly.

Morris and he looked back, but the thin grey figure was soon lost amid a crowd of people going home from work.

"Are you *sure*, Ned?" William asked. "What was his face like?"

"Yes, I saw his face clearly for a moment. His eyes were like Shelley's, just as they are in our engraving; but he looked straight through me, as if at a vision of his own. He looked shy and timid, and seemed to have a scar on his lip. *Has* he a scar?"

"Yes! Dr Ackland told me so; and he knows him! A dog bit him there when he was three."

The bell at Christ Church was tolling the curfew as they passed the Martyrs' Memorial, and beyond the stone vases of Trinity chapel a great yellow star was gleaming softly, while others were beginning to prick out in the clear dusk above them.

"I *am* glad we've seen him!" exclaimed Morris, as they stumbled along the dark, uncertain passage to Ted's rooms. There a bright fire was burning, and later, when they returned from Hall, it was in honour of having seen the writer himself that they read some passages from *The Nature of Gothic* aloud.

"Now read your poem again, Top," said Jones.

The reading had scarcely begun, however, when there was a sound of hurrying footsteps along the passage, and in came Dixon and Crom, two of Ted's old school friends.

"Dixon! Crom! He's a big poet!" cried Jones, by way of greeting.

"Who is?" asked Crom, looking round.

"Why, Topsy! You just listen! Come on, Top, read it to them! It's a perfect poem, and he's never written one before!"

They all sat down, and presently, not without some embarrassment, Morris began to read. But he was soon lost in his own images, and in the measured chant with which he always read poetry, emphasizing the rhymes, rocking his chair back and forth.

After he had finished the other two friends showed as much astonishment and appreciation as Ted had done.

"Well, if this is poetry, it's very easy to write," said Morris simply, in answer to their praises. And, from then on, hardly a day passed without some new production.

Years later, as an aged canon, Dixon was to remember with mild emotion that firelit evening, and Morris's first poem; for that room, with the old buildings of Exeter, was soon to vanish, and the poem was destroyed by Morris himself, with other sweet early works.

Chapter 9

THE SET PHILOSOPHIZES

For, in the first place, an University education fits a man about as much for being a ship-captain as a Pastor of souls: besides, your money has been by no means thrown away, if the love of friends faithful and true, friends first seen and loved here, if this love is something priceless, and not to be bought again any where and by any means: if moreover by living here and seeing evil and sin in their foulest and coarsest forms, as one does day by day, I have learned to hate any form of sin, and to wish to fight against it, is not this well too?

MORRIS, *in a letter to his mother*

THOUGH William and Edward became close friends so early, they found few others with tastes and aspirations like their own; and, except for their small circle, most of whom were old schoolfellows of Edward's, they kept very much to themselves. But as time went on this small circle became very intimate, and by the time its Oxford career was nearing its close had assumed the significant name of "the Brotherhood."

Indeed, at first the friends had shared one another's views so closely that they had seriously considered founding a kind of monastery, where they could escape together from the ugliness and distractions of nineteenth-century life, and each could work unhampered at his own calling—work, not in a selfish way, but with the good of humanity as their common aim, each using his talent—painting, writing, or whatever it might be—"for the bettering of the world as far as lay in him." And, though the monastery was never founded, and the chances of life led the friends into far

51

different paths and places, yet it may be said that this helping of the world remained truly the aim of each one all his life long.

One lovely evening of late May '55, during their next to last term at Oxford, William and Edward had strolled down to Pembroke, and found the rest of the circle already gathered in Fulford's rooms there; for Fulford, the ardent disciple of Tennyson and the most mature in intellect of the set, was a Pembroke man; as were Faulkner and Dixon, the one a brilliant mathematician, the other a future canon of the Church of England. Crom, or, to give him his full name, Cormell Price, had dropped in from Christ Church, and thus was the set complete.

" What would the Brotherhood say to a walk to Iffley? " asked Fulford, when a bottle or two of claret had been drunk and pipes were well alight. " It's far too fine to sit indoors."

The Brotherhood rose willingly, and out they went to taste to the full the joy of one another's company and the perfect sweetness of the May evening. For Oxford was a little city then, with cornfields and meadows up to its very walls; not till thirty years later was the flood of ugly houses to sweep over the willow-grown fields to the north, and not till the nineteen-thirties was Oxford to become the noisy, vulgar, industrial town that it is to-day.

Making for Iffley, they passed Christ Church and Merton by way of the meadows, and were crossing Magdalen bridge by the time the bells chimed nine from the traceried tower high above them. And once over the river, except for a tiny cluster of old houses, the country greeted them in all its beauty—the country which Matthew Arnold's *Scholar-Gipsy*, then just written, was to make so famous that many who have never seen Oxford yet love it as if they knew it well.

How white were the hedges with hemlock, cow's parsley, and foaming hawthorn (for May is the month of white flowers)! How the chestnuts towered up, aflame with newly opening snowy candles, far into the cloudless skies! And, oh, how the blackbirds sang!

To their right, through the calm meadows, where the sheep were quietly grazing, ran the great river, unseen but for the silver willow-borders which followed its windings; and far beyond them showed the faint blue lines of the Wytham hills. Up to their left rose the cornfields, green and unstirred by any wind, up to Shotover and to many a wooded hill beyond, over which the larks were singing and the moon was slowly sailing.

The friends walked in silence for a while, delighted with the beauty which was so welcome after a hard day's working for Finals. Then, Crom humming a phrase of plainsong, William took it up, in his mighty, deep voice, loud enough to fill a cathedral, till you might have thought a holy pro-cession was passing by. For they all loved the music of the Middle Ages, as they did its buildings, and had all learnt to sing it.

Meanwhile Faulkner and Ted had started talking about painting, and William broke off to join them. Faulkner said modern painting was hopelessly dull and lifeless, and William and Ted agreed with him heartily, save for one set of painters only, whose work they had lately seen, and who called them-selves the Pre-Raphaelite Brotherhood. Millais, Hunt, and Rossetti were the most prominent names of the group, and William related excitedly how he and Ted had fallen in love with their work at first sight, when they saw some small pictures of theirs at a private house at Oxford. " The *colour*! " he explained. " The colour! The brightness and the clearness and the purity of it! Like stained glass, only clearer! And the *thought* behind their work! So strongly and intensely felt, yet so utterly sincere and simple!

" They call themselves Pre-Raphaelites," he went on, " because they hold that something went wrong with painting after Raphael—people became too clever, too interested in technique; while the feeling they put into their work became shallow and insincere. So these artists want to return to the simplicity and sincerity of the Primitive painters—those of the very early Renaissance or before; and I'm sure they're right, aren't you, Ned?"

" *That* I am," Ned agreed, " and if ever I become a painter I shall take Rossetti for a master."

" So will I," said William.

Then Fulford said he too knew something of Rossetti; and he brought out a copy of a diminutive magazine he had found in Parker's that very day, called *The Germ*, and printed by these very Pre-Raphaelites in order to spread their views. And as they walked he read them a poem from it by Rossetti, who was poet as well as painter. It told of a dead maiden looking down from Paradise into the vastness of space, wondering when her lover would come to join her.

> " The blessed damozel leaned out
> From the gold bar of Heaven :
> Her blue grave eyes were deeper much
> Than a deep water, even."

it began. Fulford was a born reader, and all listened intently.

" Well," said Morris, when he had finished, " if any man's a genius, he is! "

" A fine poet, yes," said Fulford, " but not Tennyson's equal. Think of Tennyson's dignity, and the perfectly balanced music of his verse. No one can touch it to-day. Then the magic of ' Tears, idle tears '! No one can touch him or Keats for magic! "

" Not for music, perhaps, nor for magic," Morris answered, " but for imagery I think Rossetti's better. No one ever makes you *see* anything half so vividly as Rossetti does here. Tennyson has the ears, but Rossetti the eyes, and they matter most."

" But what about the heart? " interposed Dixon.

" The heart is important, yes, but the eyes come first with me. I may seem inhuman, but that's how I'm made. I value surroundings most."

" Oh, but, Topsy," objected Crom, " what are surroundings if you're miserable—if you're starving, for instance ? "

" Well, I suppose I've never been really poor, that's all," answered William simply. And, indeed, he had not; for, with his wealthy parents, he had little chance to know the hardships of the poor of those days, though later their sufferings were to make him a passionate socialist. Only this March he had come into his patrimony of nine hundred a year, and it seemed like an evil dream to him, scarcely true, when the conversation turned to the social conditions of the day, and Crom and Dixon spoke of the terrible hardships of the poor, as they had seen them in the slums of Birmingham, close to where they and Edward had been to school. Edward knew of them too, but the artist in him had shrunk from evils which he had not the power to put right, and he rarely spoke of them. But Crom told how terrible was the poverty among the working people there, who had no trade unions to protect them, but were treated like slaves by the heartless new⁄rich factory⁄owners. Most of them, he said, were starving or nearly starving, the only pleasure within their reach being to get drunk on almost poisonous spirits in the gin⁄palaces of those days!

How terrible life was! Yet what could they do to help ? Though years later Morris was to use his mature powers of tongue and pen in such tremendous efforts as a social reformer, he could see no way as yet. The talk strayed on to the horror and wickedness of the Crimean War. Only last autumn thousands had died there in the most terrible epidemic of cholera ever known in modern times.

" Why should men die ? " William asked. " Men with feelings like us, able to take pleasure in all the world's beauty, just as we do—why should they kill each other so that one nation may become a little richer or more powerful than its neighbour ? Why, you say the Middle Ages were bloodthirsty, but people nowadays are worse. A knight I wouldn't mind being, but to be dressed up in red and marched off to shoot men I don't hate, and who have done me no harm—why, I'll revolt sooner than that!"

They had been going up a steep lane, whose hedges were overgrown with wild roses and honeysuckle, and now paused where the road divided, one branch going to Iffley church, the other sloping sharply downward to the weir. The moon was bright now, and cast their shadows on the white road, as they paused in silence, uncertain as to which way to take. They listened to the rustling of the waters, and the faint wind that was just rippling the poplar leaves overhead. Fulford made as to go on to the churchyard, and the others were following, when William drew Edward back.

" Come down and look at the island," he said; " there's sure to be a nightingale or two there, if we're quiet. I love life better than death, don't you?"

Edward went with him, and, though they heard no nightingale, he long remembered the glitter of the moonlight on the aspens, and the smooth rounds of water that flowed through the weirs, which he and William watched in a half-dream till the others joined them, and the party crossed the lock to go back to Oxford by the towing-path.

On the way back plans for the coming Long Vacation were discussed—especially the projected walking tour in Northern France, which Edward, William, Fulford, and Crom had agreed to take. They were to walk for economy's sake and to avoid the noisy ugliness of trains, and were to see Chartres, Amiens, Beauvais, Rouen, all the places they had read so much about, and all the country they had read of in Froissart, and which William, who had been once before, last Long Vacation, described to them with loving vividness; for it had already begun to make the background to the poems and prose romances which he had started to write. How it thrilled Ned and Crom, neither of whom had been abroad before! They longed for it so much, they scarcely liked to speak of it, lest some irony of fate, in the form of lack of money or parental authority, might step in and prevent it!

As for William, he was his own master now, so he had no such fears. He just thought how he would write, and write, and write, as soon as he had time. And what a harvest of ideas and images the journey to France would yield! He would like *their* Brotherhood to produce something like the Pre-Raphaelite *Germ*, which Fulford had shown them to-night. And, if they did, perhaps Rossetti himself would one day let them print some of his work! Perhaps he would even know him one day as a friend! Meanwhile he would do his best to write, if not as well as Rossetti, at least as sincerely and as independently of accepted traditions as he did. And he drew fresh encouragement from the thought of following him—the encouragement of having found at last a forerunner who, like himself, esteemed the eyes far above all the other senses, even in poetry.

Chapter 10

BEAUVAIS, CHARTRES, ROUEN:
THE DECISION ON THE QUAY

Less than forty years ago, I first saw the city of Rouen, then still
in its outward aspect a piece of the Middle Ages: no words can
tell how its mingled beauty, history and romance took hold on
me; I can only say that, looking back on my past life, I find it
was the greatest pleasure I have ever had: and now it is a pleasure
which no one can ever have again: it is lost to the world for ever.

The Aims of Art

THAT'S a fine drawing, Ned! Well worth sitting on
the cobbles for and being sworn at by all the carters in
Abbeville!" In the candlelight of their low, white bedroom Jones was looking through the work of the day, and
Morris leaned over his friend's shoulder to admire the delicately
drawn tracery and pinnacles of a decorated Gothic doorway.
Jones looked up with a dreamy smile.

"On to Amiens to-morrow, and then to Beauvais—how I
long to see Beauvais, Topsy! I have a feeling that its beauty
will sweep me right away."

"If only—oh dear, if only Crom were here too!" Morris
gave a sigh. "Fulford seems happy enough to go where we
want to, but I must say I do miss Crom. If it wasn't for you,
old Ned, who see it so much as I do, I should spend every
other day writing to Crom about everything." He blew out
the candle as he spoke.

With visions of medieval carvings floating on the darkness,
Jones and Morris shouted a good-night to Fulford through the
wall, and their visions turned to dreams.

A week or so later they were in Paris, and here it was

58

Fulford's turn to show the greatest delight in everything they saw. At the Beaux Arts they found, to their delight, seven Pre-Raphaelite pictures, among these Hunt's *Light of the World* and Millais' *Order of Release*. The same evening, rather against Morris's will, they went to hear Alboni in *Le Prophète*. Jones could not hide his pleasure at the opera, though he noticed that for once Topsy was not sharing his delight. Morris had actually opposed the inclusion of Paris in their tour; his heart was set upon seeing Rouen again. He had visited that medieval city alone the summer before, and, as he was to write nearly forty years later, " No words can tell how its mingled beauty, history, and romance took hold on me." With such an experience awaiting him one can understand how the delay, the crowded, fashionable streets, the nineteenth-century atmosphere fretted him. It was with reviving spirits, then, that he at last drew his companions out into the country again, journeying by diligence, (as they had done since Morris became lame at Amiens, and had to buy a pair of carpet slippers, in which he held out for ten of the eighteen miles to Beauvais).

The great coach swung heavily along between cornfields unbounded by any hedges, sometimes over a grey bridge across a poplar-lined canal, or along lanes between loaded orchard acres. The three English youths must have been an interesting sight to their fellow-travellers: country women journeying between remote farmsteads, a bonneted young nursemaid going to her first post, a Carthusian nun, her robes worn from long pilgrimage, fingers incessantly moving on her beads as she allowed herself an occasional quick glance at Morris's wild black head, strong, square hands, restless as her own, but with such different feelings, and eyes eagerly taking note of the ever-changing landscape on either side, and it was with some relief that she met the contrastingly calm, sweet eyes of the fair youth beside this shouting young foreigner. For Morris *had* to express his thoughts, *and* get them to Ted's ears, through the considerable rattling and rumbling and high patois chatter. Ted was content to listen to his friend's vivid, hurried words, sharing mutely in the enthusiasm that compelled them. They were so much alike in mind, these two, it seemed to need but one to speak what both were feeling.

Fulford, on the other side of Jones, was occupied with Tennysonian thoughts of his own, together with the contemplation of his opposite neighbour; for the young nursemaid, with her slender, plump figure, and blushing glances under the straw bonnet, filled his head with poetic phrases that had to be wasted because of the impossibility of writing them down in this confounded diligence. *Here* was the "Gardener's Daughter"; here was a vision of greater worth than all their churches and cathedrals, did these two but know it! He, Fulford, knew it, and couldn't record even a line! Ah, Tennyson! That voice was the greatest that would ever sound! Nothing further of worth would ever be written after the Master's voice was stilled!

Suddenly Morris startled the whole company by a great shout. All who could hastened to look where he was pointing.

Out to the east, beyond a line of poplars shimmering in the last brightness of sunlight, flashed gilded vanes and silver pinnacles above a cluster of steep roofs. As the coach slowed down at a toll-bridge the faint chiming of bells came to their ears over the quiet, long-shadowed wheat-land.

" C'est seulement Chartres que vous voyez là-bas, seulement la ville de Chartres, messieurs! " said one of the country women reassuringly. What could have startled the gentleman in such an ordinary sight!

But Morris gazed, lost in his imaginings, at the nearing spires, until the coach turned full towards them, and ten minutes later rattled over the first cobbles and drew up in the colonnaded courtyard of a large hostel.

For the next few days, while Jones was drawing traceried doorways or early fragments in various parts of the old town, alone or with Fulford, Morris wandered everywhere, in and around the great cathedral, his eyes taking in each detail, naming each architectural part with unconscious scholarship, till Fulford marvelled at his utter knowledge, and tried to learn from him. But Morris's knowledge of medievalism, in all its surviving forms, was deep-planted, infallible, as if it had always been there, in his mind—and perhaps it had. Certainly none could ever remember seeing him reading books on it since those early days in the library at Marlborough.

Even the subject of Tennyson was allowed to rest, on these walks. But, as often, Morris would go alone out of the town, across the thickly flowered meadows, and mint-filled streams, to some place from where he could look back at Chartres at its best, across wide expanses of bowed wheat-ears, or above thin, ever-changing poplar-trees. For hours he would wander round and about, seeking the perfect prospect of this ancient splendour and August loveliness, till peasants at work over their scythes called to one another that he must have lost his mind, and crossed themselves solemnly.

Presently, though, it was time to continue their journey. Morris was panicked lest they should have to return to Paris to reach Rouen, and at that by train. But they made inquiries, and finally arranged to go by train across country to Maintenon, whence they continued by carriage for some way. Chartres was veiled in a mist of fine rain, the cathedral spires almost invisible, high up in the grey dawn light, as they left at six in the morning.

The country was filled with changing lights, most beautiful under the steady rain. Morris was enraptured with the wealth of all this beauty; he felt that he must pour out the images in the stories that were forming in his mind, as soon as he got back to Oxford. They reached Evreux, having had to endure a brief train journey, in time to have dinner. Morris finished his quickly, and went alone to look at the cathedral; more penetrating eyes, such a craftsman's mind, could not have

contemplated those airy traceries, glowing windows, and flying canopies for many a day.

As far as Louviers, the last town before Rouen, they
travelled by road through wooded valleys, widely planted
orchards, fields a-sway with meadow flowers. The last five
miles to the railway station were made in low sunlight, which
flooded across the wide valley behind them and over the river,
lengthening the shadows of great trees grouped along it in the
deep-flowered grass, until it seemed to Morris an ideal setting
for pastoral romance or one of Chaucer's most delicate tales.

But alas for the actual arrival into Rouen town! His
indignant words written to dearest Crom, when the tour was
almost over, sound in our ears as if he were speaking here, now!

> But we had to leave it [the Arcadian valley] and go to Rouen by a
> nasty, brimstone, noisy, shrieking railway train that cares not two-
> pence for hill or valley, poplar tree or lime tree, corn poppy or blue
> cornflower, or purple thistle and purple vetch, white convolvulus,
> white clematis, or golden St John's wort; that cares not twopence
> either for tower or spire, or apse, or dome, for it will be as noisy and
> obtrusive under the spires of Chartres or the towers of Rouen, as it is
> under Versailles or the Dome of the Invalides; verily railways are
> ABOMINATIONS; and I think I have never fairly realised this fact till
> this our tour: fancy, Crom, all the roads (or nearly all) that come
> into Rouen dip down into the valley where it lies, from gorgeous hills
> that command the most splendid views of Rouen, but we, coming
> into Rouen by railway, crept into it in the most seedy way, seeing
> actually nothing at all of it until we were driving through the town
> in an omnibus.
>
> I had some kind of misgivings that I might have been disappointed
> with Rouen, after my remembrances of it from last year, but I wasn't
> a bit. O! what a place it is.

The gradual approach of such a dreamlike wandering to
ordinary life again, as it nears its end, brings a certain weight
of depression on the mind so lately exulting. Fulford will
have felt this weight, and expressed it in a lost Tennysonian
fragment. Morris and Jones, however, shared thoughts and

feelings so momentous that no other emotion could concern them.

Through the past weeks, as their souls were expanding more and more to all the beauty they were seeing, in each separately a self-knowledge was growing. On their last night in France, as they walked together hour on hour upon the deserted quay at Havre, the water beside them scarcely audible, so still an August night it was, they talked of many serious things, and at last confessed to each other this new-found truth.

Morris spoke quietly: " Ned, I cannot be a clergyman. It would be wrong, without heart and soul wanting to. And mine never really did. It was the unearthly beauty of visible worship that I loved—not the urge to pastor souls."

" Oh, I am glad you've said that at last! " Jones pressed his friend's arm in a flood of affection and gladness. " For days I have been wanting to tell you what came to me in Beauvais, after you and Fulford left me. Top, I'm going to be an artist, a painter of pictures that will fill those who look at them with such happiness as we've known these last few weeks! I shall dedicate my life to painting the Beautiful, as soon as I can begin."

" And I shall take up architecture. There is a good man in Oxford with whom I can start working. It'll be nice to stay on in the old town, but we must keep firm, this next term, *and* when we go home, against all persuasions and threats that may be used to weaken our resolves. And after all, Ned, it *is* our own lives that we are planning! And no one else is going to suffer in the end, if we're mistaken, but ourselves! Come, let's make it a vow here, in the last few moments of this wonderful vacation, to remain firm in our resolves, encourage each other, *and* work *hard* from now on! "

The vow was made, with clasped hands and momentary silence. Then they walked towards the distant, lighted gang-way, and mounted with the earliest passengers to the deck above.

Chapter 11

ROSSETTI

This is her picture as she was:
  It seems a thing to wonder on,
As though mine image in the glass
  Should tarry when myself am gone.

ROSSETTI, The Portrait

" Under the arch of Life, where love and death,
Terror and mystery, guard her shrine, I saw
Beauty enthroned; and though her gaze struck awe,
  I drew it in as simply as my breath.
  Hers are the eyes which, over and beneath,
The sky and sea bend on thee, — which can draw,
By sea or sky or woman, to one law,
  The allotted bondman of her palm and wreath.

" This is that Lady Beauty, in whose praise
  Thy voice and hand shake still, — long known to thee
By flying hair and fluttering hem, — the beat
Following her daily of thy heart and feet,
  How passionately and irretrievably,
  In what fond flight, how many ways and days!"

The powerful Southern voice ceased, and the reader rose to
return to a drawing that rested on an easel near by—a young
girl's head, pensive, drooping. Before it reclined the girl herself; and now she stirred and poised her head, ready to be
drawn again.

" Rossetti, in that sonnet you have said most perfectly what
Ted and I have been feeling consciously for nearly a year—
and unconsciously for all our lives, I believe, don't you,
Ted?"

Morris turned to Burne-Jones[1] as he finished. The latter was looking very tired, from long days at the easel and long nights in converse, here in Rossetti's studio, or visited by his guide and master in his own rooms. He was thinner, too, since the summer in France. But he answered fervently, " I do; you know I do, Top! Goodness, how lucky we are to have one another in this approaching crusade for the beauty that used to be—and you to lead us, Rossetti! If the power is in me I couldn't fail, led and inspired by you! "

The older man smiled kindly as he went on with his drawing. Even through his careless, paint-soiled clothes, neglected black locks, unconscious growth of beard, even in spite of the hopeless, unalterable disorder of the great studio, there glowed a radiance that permeated all around him—a radiance of perfect conviction in his own high powers and judgment, in the values he held and preached.

" Morris should be an artist too," he said presently.

The dark head looked up quickly. " How do you know, Rossetti? "

" All men who have the soul, the eyes, for the world's beauty should portray it for the rest of mankind, who can only see it through them. The painter and the buyer of paintings—those are the only two classes of people who ought to exist! "

" But how can I know whether I am a painter, without wasting many years in learning to paint? Architecture so far hasn't proved over-interesting—but I must progress with some-thing definite."

Rossetti laid down his pencil and crossed to a pile of draw-ings on the floor. Kneeling down, he searched swiftly through them, then drew out what he had been looking for. It was a simple pastel drawing of an angel's head, aureole-crowned, the glance set patiently on something far away behind the beholder,

---

[1] About this time Burne Jones hyphenated his surname.

the light, massed hair caught back by a scallop-shell. The eyes were grey and sad as sea waves.

He handed it to Morris. " If you can find time in the week, I should like you to take this back and try to do a copy of it. I'll give you a piece of sanguine before you go." Morris thanked him fervently, and said he would try to do his best to make something of a copy. But as he contemplated the drawing his slight hope of success ebbed away. It was so perfectly skilled and masterly, he foresaw his own effort making him want to weep with exasperation and defeat.

" However, I will do the best I can, and bring the miserable result to face your scorn next Sunday!" he said aloud.

" Don't be quite so despondent, Mr Morris!" said the girl, smiling across at him. " I'll tell you something that will surprise you into having more hopes of yourself—I am a painter too, and simply through Gabriel's teaching, so you won't need to bring any talent when you come and learn with him! *I* didn't—*he* will tell you that!"

" That's nonsense, Lizzie—you brought all the desire, and *that* is talent. But you haven't told them whom you gained as patron of this pretty talent of yours!"

Miss Siddal coloured faintly, but the young men urged her to tell them, so at length she said, " Well, he isn't really my patron, he's Gabriel's, but he helps me for Gabriel's sake, so he shouldn't be worried about my having no money; he's Mr Ruskin, you see, Gabriel's friend and admirer. But he pays me a great deal—a hundred and fifty pounds a year for all I do."

Burne-Jones was about to ask her to show them some of her pictures, when she turned to the window and exclaimed, "Why, the light's showing through the shutters; it must be day!"

Morris leapt up, and glanced at his new hunter, worn since the confinement to regular office hours.

" Thank you for saying that, Miss Siddal," he exclaimed. " I must find a cab at once, or that train will be missed!"

"A piece of paper to put round the drawing! And the chalk!" cried Burne-Jones, running to the heaped bureau.

The picture was quickly rolled up, chalk wrapped in handkerchief, and with a hasty farewell Morris stumbled down several dark flights and out into the silent street.

To his great relief, a hansom turned the corner and came ambling down towards him. The horse-hoofs echoed chilly in the waning gaslight. Morris roared to it to stop, and was presently swaying along to Paddington, half asleep.

How greyly day seems to begin when one has made day of the previous night! Morris entered Street's small, orderly office with a heart distinctly hostile to the work of Monday morning. Young Webb was there, already bent over ruler and pencil.

"He's just been asking if you're here," he said, seeing Morris.

Morris hung up his coat carefully, Rossetti's drawing hidden down one of the sleeves.

"Well, I'm not late this morning. Where's the foundation for the church he wants drawn out? Why can't people build churches as they used to, without all this drawing and planning to scale! All the spirit of the building is gone by the time each stone has been numbered! Beauvais and Chartres were not made in that way! I never thought architecture meant a life-time of this kind of thing!"

The grumbles ceased as he held his breath for a slow, straight line, and young Philip Webb quelled the faint stirrings of discontent that Morris's words sometimes roused in him.

Chapter 12

RED LION SQUARE

"Wulf, I will teach you painting now, come and learn." Then
I tried to learn painting till I thought I should die, but at last I
learnt it through much pain and grief.

The Hollow Land

THE rooms at 17 Red Lion Square to which Morris
and Burne-Jones moved at the beginning of '57 were
let unfurnished. The thought of buying the ready-
made furniture of the time was intolerable to both of them, so
they set themselves to making rough designs to suit their
strongly medieval tastes, and had these converted into reality
by a small carpenter in the neighbourhood. Gradually the
things appeared, and began to fill their large studio room:
first a table, large, round, "as firm and heavy as a rock," then
several heavy, rough-hewn chairs, "such as Barbarossa might
have sat in!"

But their most ambitious piece was yet to arrive, and all
their talk was of it—where it should stand, how it should be
embellished—as the two young artists hurried back, one wild
March evening, through the wind-swept Bloomsbury streets.
As the gust bellowed against them round the last corner
Morris rejoiced secretly for a moment to think that his grey
ulster and purple trousers were as inadequate against the bitter
wind as his friend's clothes. Deliberately he had left at Water
House all such clothes as would show him to be richer than
Burne-Jones, for, equal in mind, he wished also to be equal
in fortune as far as might be, to forget his luxurious income of
nine hundred a year, unless he was spending it as Rossetti
directed, in buying the pictures of other worthy artists.

A minute after their arrival home the place was in an uproar. For there, stuck fast midway up the narrow stairs, they found their proudest effort, doors a-swing and almost upended, the carpenter and his man quite unable to move it another inch up or down.

"Perhaps you gave the measurements a bit too big, Top," Ted's voice sounded plaintively amid the storm of maledictions that Morris, distracted by defeat and disappointment, was hurling at the helpless carpenter and at every carpenter in the world. But the mild reproach in Ted's voice struck home, and Morris abruptly turned his energies to putting things right: calling on those above to pull for their lives, he pushed from below with a bull's strength, aided presently by the hefty shoulders of Red Lion Mary, maid-of-all-work, always glad to leave her mopping for a more diverting occupation. And now, with her strength added, the day was won, and before long, to Morris's infinite satisfaction, there it stood, noble and steady as a cliff (Morris always insisted that furniture should be steady), and filling almost a third of their studio.

"Well, I think it's jolly, don't you, Ned?"

"Yes, Topsy, I really think it is, even if it *is* a bit big."

"A bit big? Nonsense, Ned! You wait till Gabriel sees it; he'll want to paint those panels, I can tell you. That's why I had them made big."

"I'll want to paint *what*?" asked a cheerful voice, as none other than Gabriel himself marched into the room. "Well, Top, you've gone the whole hog this time. It's a settle, I suppose, though the cupboards up top look a bit odd. Quite out of reach, of course, unless you're going to keep flying pets— owls, are they? But let's have some charcoal." And, sure enough, he began to draw, delighted with the smooth, pale wood of the panels, a design for a painting of angels standing a-row, with flaming hair, and singing, and playing on ancient musical instruments. Topsy and Ned watched in silent admiration.

"I told you so, Ned," Topsy whispered.

"Yes, you're right. And it makes me want to do the same. Make me a wardrobe, Top, and I'll paint it all over for you with scenes from Chaucer, and angels even lovelier than Gabriel's."

"Lovelier they couldn't be, Ned, but the cupboard you shall have."

And, not long after, the famous Chaucer wardrobe was finished, which stood in William's drawing-room all his life, and now rests in the Ashmolean Museum at Oxford, as a perfect example of William and Edward's early collaboration. And many other pieces did they create together—pianos, stained-glass windows, tapestries—but more of these in their appointed place.

Meanwhile in came Mary with their roast pork, the smell of which made them all forget art for a while, even though the crackling *was* a little overdone, owing to the vicissitudes of the day. As they ate, Gabriel said he had brought some news which was of the first importance. "A commission for you both which you absolutely must accept—the chance of a lifetime. You know the Union at Oxford has a new debating-hall—Ruskin's had a lot to do with it—well, the walls are to be frescoed, and I'm going to do it, with subjects from the *Morte d'Arthur*—though they're only paying my expenses—no fee. But it's such a splendid chance; the work will be world-famous and everlasting; so tell me you'll help me, for it'll take ten men at least to do it, the first two of whom are going to be you, Ned, and you, Topsy."

"But I've had no experience—I'm not good enough," stammered Topsy. "My work would look awful beside yours."

"And mine too," said Burne-Jones.

But Gabriel swept their hesitations away. "You two have more poetry in you than anyone else I know, and to have the stuff in you is the first essential. Don't fear for the rest—just do your sincere best, and I'll see that you don't fail. You, Top, are a born designer, whatever your limitations may be in figure-drawing, and I mean you to do the decorations of the roof. So not a word more against it. Promise me you'll come."

" All right, Gabriel, we will," they both promised.

And straightway they began to plan the cycle of paintings which, had fortune been kinder and their knowledge of painting chemistry better, would have been for centuries a wonder of the world for simple beauty and fresh sincerity of endeavour.

Chapter 13

THE MURALS AT OXFORD

Tall she was and slender . . . her hair dark brown and
plenteous, her eyes grey, her chin round and lovely, her cheeks a
little hollow, and in the hollow of them entreaty and all entice-
ment: she stood looking shyly at the newcomer . . . and he
scarce knew where he was, but looked down on the floor, as
though the Sundering Flood of the Dales rolled betwixt him and
the maiden; for indeed when his eyes first fell upon her he knew
that it was Elfhild.

The Sundering Flood

OUTSIDE the lofty, newly completed hall of the
Union, August heat beat down on Oxford towers,
fading the lichened stone to an even paler silver. But,
inside, the six young artists who had come up to Oxford a
few days before were impervious to anything but the sweep
of their huge brushes, as they worked away high up on their
platforms, above the bookshelves and gallery that ran round
on all sides of the hall.

There were ten wall-spaces to be covered, four bays between
the roof-groins on either side, and two apsidal ends. These
bays were each pierced by two circular windows. The surface
was just as the builders had left it, except for a coat of white-
wash, and the mortar was hardly dry. None of the young artists
had any knowledge of fresco painting, nor, fortunately, did they
know what a dismal failure their happy labours were so soon
to become. So each worked on, lost in the subject of his picture.

And who were they? What were these pictures? The
artists' names are now variously familiar or obscure. The
subjects were ten scenes from Malory's *Morte d'Arthur*.

72

Presently Morris, who had been working away rapidly for the last two hours, put down his brushes, and announced with a shout of joy that he had finished! He had raced ahead of his friends, it is true, beginning his painting on the wall before Burne-Jones or Rossetti had even completed their designs; but even so they heard his shout of joy with surprise, and presently Rossetti came along the narrow gallery beneath, palette in hand, to look at the result. A few tense moments passed, then the clear Italian voice sounded in Morris's ears—and made him want to dash out at once the row of tall bright sunflowers behind which the sorrowful Sir Palomides walked.

"Bravely done, bravely done, my friend! And very fine sunflowers they are too! Now you might help out Stanhope with his foreground by filling it up with scarlet runners for him!"

There was a general laugh, but Morris turned away with a frown, and, silently gathering up his paints, went down to the hall. A moment before he had been so elated, and quite in love with that row of staring flower-heads. Now he could only growl with anger. In this mood he was just about to revenge his wounded feelings on the door as he passed through, when a small, swarthy figure appeared, coming along the passage, carrying something that clanked and rang at every step.

It was the little blacksmith from Quaking Bridge. As Morris strode up to him he threw down his burden for him to see—a shining helmet with visor and mail coif, a broad-bladed, heavy-pommelled sword, and a long Norman shield.

Morris leapt on the pile, and all his crossness vanished as he unlatched the helmet and put it over his head. The smith fastened it on, not without some expressions of satisfaction at his strange new creation. Sword and shield were handed to him, and there he stood, like his own Sir Palomides. But his pleasure in these knightly objects could not be expressed standing still. With clash of sword on shield and a challenging shout he leapt and charged about the passage, crashing his

73

helmet from side to side, until the smith departed in fear for his own safety. But after several victorious bouts he was filled with the desire to see the magnificent helmet again, in a better light; he stumbled through into the hall and tried to remove it. But, against growing struggles and growls of impatience, the helmet remained firmly closed. He began to stamp, and finally to bellow and roar and lurch about, filling the place with such a clamour that even Burne-Jones was called back to earth mentally and bodily, and, running to him, helped to ease off the helmet, with a few tufts of strong black hairs.

And what a face struggled out of the depths of it! Scarlet, panting, still heaping imprecations on the little blacksmith, Morris stood glowering at all around, until his sense of humour suddenly returned, and he joined in the general mirth at his own absurdity. Then, to prove that he was really him-self again, he proposed that they should cease work for the day, and go and have some iced cider-punch at the King's Arms. Taking Burne-Jones by the arm, he led him out into the warm airs of St Michael's Street, and down Ship Street, into the Broad.

It was pleasingly cool in the low room they presently entered, and though the window looked out merely into Holy-well, level with all who passed by, they ranged their chairs about it, glad of a slight breeze, and were soon draining long draughts of the heady amber punch.

"Ted told me you saw a great sight at the theatre last night," said Morris to Rossetti presently; "two beauties that were sitting in front of you both—and he said you actually managed to speak to them afterwards. Tell us more about it?"

"Well, I saw at once that one was an absolute stunner— wide, calm, grey eyes, perfect mouth, and full dark hair— such a face as turns a man giddy to see. I shall try to get her father to let her sit to me. He's a reputable saddler, 'some-where in Oxford,' so she said, when I begged leave to call on her formally, but she wouldn't give the address. But I'll find it somehow, and if they consent I'll draw as if from one of heaven's own angels! She had hands shaped to rest on virginals or work pictures in tapestry! Ned noticed them at once."

Suddenly light voices and a glimpse of dark hair and fluttering lawn passed by the open window.

" The stunner! " cried Burne-Jones, leaping up. " Quick, Gabriel, see where she goes! " And he ran out and round the corner into Holywell, followed by all except Morris, who delayed to pay for their drinks. The five pursuers had surrounded their quarry some way down the street, when he came in sight of them. Rossetti's captivating speech and Burne-Jones's earnest admiration had won the two young girls to linger for a moment, to recall the meeting of the previous evening, and they were immediately surrounded by five, and presently six, admiring pairs of eyes, and five voices vied in polite addresses. Five, for Morris stood without a word. His eyes were resting on the taller girl's face, watching every turn and glance, as she replied with shy gravity to Rossetti's impulsive questions.

Later that evening, in Morris's rooms, as Burne-Jones rose to leave, his friend's unusually silent mood during the whole evening prompted him to ask whether he had received any worrying news, or had been offended in any way.

" Oh, no, nothing like that, Ned! " replied Morris, smiling at his friend's anxious face. " But I will tell *you* alone of all people, if it *is* what I believe it to be. But you mustn't be anxious, for it can only be either nothing at all or else something very wonderful, but of which we have never before spoken or thought."

So they bade each other good night. But many, many thoughts and images passed through Morris's mind before he could fall asleep, and all the next day he could not free himself from the remembrance of that beautiful, wide-eyed countenance.

At the end of the week Morris was hard at work anew, this time on a platform high up among the roof-ribs, for he had been allowed to undertake the decoration of the ceiling spaces between the vaulting beams, and the design of flowers for it had been but the work of one day for the extraordinary youth.

All through the autumn he worked on at the ceiling, helped sometimes by Charles Faulkner, who came and filled the foliage with strange beasts and birds, and here and there a caricature of Morris himself. Many were brought in to admire the bright, dreamlike scenes that glowed now among the dark groins; bright sweet colours and shapes, Rossetti's *Vision of the Sangrael* the fairest of all, though never finished after he was called away by Elizabeth Siddal's illness.

One day Val Prinsep brought in a thin, elfin personage with a mop of flaming red hair that surpassed Morris's in startlingness. He was up at Balliol, and had a reputation for dazzling converse and poetic genius. Morris saw him from his perch high up on the rafters, and liked the look of him; and soon after they were introduced, by Edwin Hatch of Pembroke, and Morris liked him more, and revealed his own poetic genius, even reading to him some of the poems he was preparing to publish. They won from the strange, wild youth floods of extravagant praise, and later the greater compliment of imitation.

Chapter 14

THUNDER IN THE GARDEN

For her smile was of longing, no longer of glee,
   And her fingers, entwined with mine own,
With caresses unquiet sought kindness of me
   For the gift I never had known.

Then down rushed the rain, and the voice of the thunder
   Smote dumb all the sound of the street,
And I to myself was grown but a wonder,
   As she leaned down my kisses to meet.

That she craved for my lips that had craved her so often,
   And the hand that had trembled to touch,
That the tears filled her eyes that I hoped not to soften
   In this world was a marvel too much.

Thunder in the Garden

WHEN all that could be done without Rossetti had been completed the other artists departed. But Morris lingered on in Oxford, and just after his twenty-fourth birthday his first book of poems was published—poems which are full of the imagery of the hornbeam glades of his childhood, the medieval magic of Oxford and of Northern France, and with the romance which had always enchanted his imagination. And through several of the most beautiful of these moves the slender, dark-haired, grey-eyed girl whom it is not difficult to recognize as Jane Burden. For during the past year she had become his beloved, and his ideal of perfect beauty. Yet, naturally shy, it was long before he could speak to anyone, even Ned, of his feelings, in spite of his promise. He was now a regular visitor at the saddler's small, neat home in Holywell, and all the time his love for the daughter grew, until at last he summoned the courage to speak to Jane's father, who, to his immense relief, was not opposed to the match.

He stayed to tea that day at the Burdens', and afterwards Jane took him out into the garden. Small and set between lofty walls of crumbling stone, where the snapdragon and white daisies grew, it reminded Morris of one of those miniature Gardens of Paradise, so beloved by the artists of the illuminated books which he adored. And as Jane passed before him between the beds full of summer flowers, where the tall red lilies were all at their best, and the stock was loud with the humming of bees, she seemed like some queen in those times of legendary beauty, herself almost as legendary, so that he trembled at the import of the question he was about to ask, the hope within him fighting all the time with a dreadful fear, when he remembered that never yet had she shown anything beyond a shy liking for him. What if this were but the kindness she seemed to show towards every one? What if his hope were only the most dreadful vanity and presumption? Well, he'd know the worst this very day, and if he failed would bear it as best he could, without complaining to a single soul, not even Ned. Indeed, he felt thankful he had told no one about his love, for then he would have no pity to endure if he failed.

All the afternoon the sky had been imperceptibly darkening, and as he looked up the great cloud-mountains that towered over them seemed all but falling. As they neared the end of the long, narrow garden great drops of rain had begun to fall, pattering heavily upon the leaves of the ancient fig-tree, which a sudden wind had set ominously rustling.

" Oh, dear," she said, " what a pity! Come, we'll have to go in."

" Oh, please not! " said William. " Here—come in here. I've something I must say to you now."

He drew her by the hand into the little summer-house,

which the heavy creepers made almost dark, and they sat there together while the rain poured down, and the thunder that had held off for so long roared out triumphantly overhead.

Between two of its loudest peals William said quickly, "Janey, I *must* know something. It's been on my mind for a very long time, and I can't bear not knowing any longer. I feel as if my very life depended on it; so tell me now—do you *like* me, because I *love* you, and *have* loved you ever since we first met?"

For some seconds she did not answer, and as he glanced fearfully to see how she had taken his confession he saw, to his dismay, that her head was turned away, and that her shoulders were trembling. In a panic he cried, "Oh, Janey, what is it? Are you angry with me?" But she only shook her head without looking round, so he cried out again, "Oh, Janey, *tell* me, only tell me, what do you mean!"

When at last she turned slowly he could see by the fitful lightning that she was smiling, as well as crying. Bowing her head, she let him draw her towards him, till he held her so closely that each felt the strong pounding of the other's heart. He dared to ask, "Is it *true*? Janey, oh, my darling, tell me, is it possibly true? Can you love me—possibly? Can you actually *love* me? Oh, my dearest Janey, tell me is it really *possible*?"

"Yes, William, I do," she whispered.

And she wept again, and so did he, as she told him how she too had loved him since long ago—since soon after they first met.

"Oh, Janey, it's too good; I can't believe it. Could you really think of *marrying* me? If you do I'll make you the loveliest home that was ever made for anyone."

"Yes, William, with all my heart—if Father and Mother consent; and I believe they will."

"They *do*, Janey! They do! I asked your father to-day, and that was why I dared ask you."

So all was well, and the doubts of these last months melted away like a dream. Their engagement was arranged to last a year, which William spent wandering restlessly between Oxford, London, and his mother's new home at Leyton, wondering how he could ever bear the waiting, demanded by Jane's scrupulous parents, but to him merely a waste of a year of life and youth which could never be made up—a year in which who knew what misfortune might happen, to mar all the happiness he hoped for!

In the summer he made a short excursion with Webb and Faulkner by boat down the Seine, coming back loaded with beautiful things for the home that was to be. At last, on the 26th of April '59, in the little church of St Michael's, Oxford, Dixon, newly ordained, read the marriage service over them, and William's mind was at rest at last.

Chapter 15

RED HOUSE FOUND AND LOST

I know a little garden-close
Set thick with lily and red rose,
Where I would wander if I might
From dewy dawn to dewy night,
And have one with me wandering.
The Life and Death of Jason

MORRIS'S greatest wish now was to begin creating as soon as possible a perfect setting for his beautiful wife: the most perfect house imaginable for them to live in, away from a world that was becoming increasingly hideous to anyone who saw or thought.

His friend Philip Webb, no longer working under Street, agreed to make the plans to his design, and to help find the ideal setting for it. One fine day in August '59 they went off together to Upton, in Kent, to see some orchard land that was

F   81

for sale near Bexley Heath. Directly he saw it Morris felt that he had found the right place at last. Clearly, as if it were already there, he imagined his house set in the midst of apple, and cherry-trees, white blossoms blowing over it in spring-time, and in the autumn laden branches leaning in at the windows; always the rustling of branches around them, and dappled shadows on the lawns. Their search was over, he announced to Webb joyfully, and took back to Janey a pocket full of red apples, as a token that the place was already theirs.

What a long time of waiting it seemed while the builders wrought on the house! But at length the time for them to move in did arrive, and it was a brilliant summer day, not quite a year after the finding of the site.

As soon as the treasures he had gradually been collecting were safely landed and found unbroken, William and Janey wandered off hand in hand all over their new house and garden, delighted with everything. And they had reason to be pleased, for Philip Webb had made full use of his gift for simple, spacious construction. His plain and cheerful red brick and tiles were in direct defiance of the then prevailing fashion of ornamented stucco and dull grey slate. L-shaped in plan, its appearance was almost Gothic, especially in the noble sweep of the open roof above the main staircase, rising to its high louvre and spirelet, and in the tall, oast-house-like roof that crowned the well-house. Inside, the most beautiful room was that in the corner of the L, with its view over the open country northward, and its western oriel over what was to be the bowling-green.

As they stood in it now William's eyes flashed like one inspired, as he said, " I'm going to make this room the most beautiful one in England! Janey, my love, these long fingers shall embroider glorious things for its adorning. Ned must paint some legend all around above your blossoming hangings; Philip must make us fine yet simple furniture—tables and chairs and chests and glass—and Gabriel shall add a treasure or two of *his* mind too! And I! Oh, Janey! I think once I start, the rich bright thoughts will pour out of my mind without end! In a thousand shapes, and such colours! And all to show how utterly I love Earth's beauty, and you, Janey mine—who are to me the essence of it all!"

He raised her serene face to look into her eyes, eyes that still made heart faint to see, and laid his lips on hers, almost reverently. Her long lashes brushed his cheek. He was lost for a space to all else, in the heavenly world of her face.

The first Christmas at Red House passed by, leaving those who shared it with Janey and William the richer in happy memories. Their closest friends continued to be their regular week-end visitors. Through snowstorm, rain, wind, wildest weather, the journey to Red House was made just as gladly.

On the 18th of January, '61, a day of calm snow-light, glancing on walls and ceiling, Janey lay gazing with wonder at her first-born child.

All their friends were invited to the christening, which was done at the small church of Bexley Heath. To accommodate every one had been no easy matter, and beds were made up all about the drawing-room for the men, the young poet Alger-non Swinburne defeating Rossetti in a contest for the sofa!

Rain and wind beat against the crowded wagonettes as they splashed along, covers flapping like sails, each bearing a laughing company. The dinner that followed was long re-called as one of especial magnificence and gaiety. Rossetti sat at the laden board like a Borgian prince, and at once began to eat his nuts and raisins, shouting between mouthfuls into the general clamour. His opponent for the sofa, warmed with steaming rum punch, soon vied with the great man again in a flow of brilliant thoughts and images, shaking back the bright red locks from his pale face.

Several subjects at once were in progress of discussion—each with its fountain-head. At the top of the table Morris, short black locks at their wildest, flashing looks from side to side as his words tumbled out fast and furiously, was launching a wild vituperation against Victorian taste in general; lower down Madox Brown was well away on his favourite subject, the Pre-Raphaelite Brotherhood; across the upper table Burne-Jones led a more controlled discussion on Romantic pictures, not without sly jokes now and then; while at the opposite end a heated argument was going on between Webb and the usually mild Faulkner about the merits of some recent Ruskin lecture; and finally, beautiful and calm as some fabled queen at a tournament, sat Janey herself, admired and encouraged, as in a quiet, half-shy way she related some incidents of her own childhood, passed amid influences of simple piety, in sight of spires and sound of bells.

The christening festivities over, William and Janey, and little Jane, or Jenny, as she soon became, lived on their perfect life, busy with countless improvements about house and garden.

But all this was the prelude to something that was destined greatly to shape the rest of their lives. One fine evening in April Janey descended from the night nursery, having given three-month-old Jenny her good-night kiss, and joined William and their week-end visitors as they strolled in the garden. As she came up to them she heard William saying, "And Janey could have women working under her; she is really a great artist in her needlework."

As she took his arm the others turned at once and told her about Gabriel's inspiration. They were to form a firm, Topsy, Ned, Gabriel, Webb, Madox Brown, and as many of the others as wished to when they heard about it; and the idea would be to design, and make or get made, everything in the way of furniture and decorations for houses and churches. They talked on until the shadows darkened around them, and a wind stirred in the white boughs and chilly, scented air. Then they went in, and resumed talk in the candle-lit drawing-room, until the leaping flames of dying tapers stirred Janey's worsted flowers to life on the dark blue hangings, and warned them to bed.

Very soon after this the scheme had become a firm, with an impressively sounding name and a capital of a hundred and nine pounds. Rossetti had composed a circular, telling of the aims and abilities of Morris, Marshall, Faulkner and Co. The language was strong, typical of the writer in its absolute self-confidence, the import of it being that commercial art had so much deteriorated that a group of established artists had at last united, with the intention of using their talents to revive good taste.

The circular gained some response, and orders began to arrive at the small London office, not without some help given by Morris's former tutor, Mr Guy. Burne-Jones was asked to supply designs for several stained-glass windows. Webb was chosen to make designs for some table-glass and furniture. Various manufacturers agreed to carry out their designs, and by the following spring their firm was enough established to be represented at that year's Exhibition.

In March of that year a second daughter was born, and christened Mary, to be known as May.

For Morris life seemed complete—home, wife, children, pleasant work. The bursts of wild rage that used to possess him, and on which his friends had long looked as an entertainment, now occurred but rarely. One shattered door-panel was the only damage to which his impetuous temperament had driven him for a whole year. And now that his designs could be carried out by suitable manufacturers, the promise made to Janey, the first day they arrived, would soon be fulfilled; their home furnished with all needful things, and those fair to see and good to use.

In the following year his first patterns for wall-papers were made; the first the " Rose Trellis," then the " Daisy," then the

" Pomegranate." The stream had started to flow, as he had foretold, and with fast-gathering strength; and soon he turned anew to writing, as a second course through which his creative powers might flow. Though ultimately never published, the unfinished epic on the fall of Troy, written at this time, shows in every line of the surviving fragments his genius for word-painting, his Greek-like sparing of all but needful words. And he was not yet in his twenty-ninth year.

Life had been so happy these last years that Morris felt sometimes that the Gods were favouring him too much, and that some day—when he knew not—his fortune must change. It gave him a sickening fear, even in the midst of his present joyfulness. Nor was his foreboding vain, for one drenching evening, when he had sat for two hours on the journey home with soaked feet and head, he went to bed with a high temperature, which not long afterwards developed into rheumatic fever.

Week after week he lay in bed, his anxiety about the firm growing ever greater; for his private income, now that the miraculous copper-mine was showing signs of being worked out, had begun alarmingly to shrink, till he realized with consternation that he and Janey and the children might soon be dependent on the firm for their means of life. So unless it was put very swiftly upon a sounder footing, and was turned into a paying concern instead of a speculation, things might go very badly with them indeed. And as he realized that it would be long before he would be well enough to make the daily journeys again—if, indeed, he ever would be—the dreadful truth began to force itself upon him: he would have to give up Red House, and go and live in London.

At first he made desperate plans for moving the firm to Upton instead, and had asked Burne-Jones to come and live there and work under one roof with him. But Burne-Jones's position as a painter was not yet firmly enough established to allow him to afford to leave London, however much he may

have wished to; so he had to refuse. And similar considera-
tions regarding the prospects of the firm made Morris finally
abandon the plan as hopeless.

As he lay in bed, weak as a child, and the rain and storm
swept pitilessly past outside, making the dusk far earlier than
its wont, he wondered how he was going to bear to leave the
Paradise that he and Janey and all their friends had made
together; he wondered and found no answer, for it seemed
like death itself. " If only I could die," he groaned to himself,
and the rain and wind outside seemed to mock him, crying,
" Die, die⁄e, die⁄e⁄e!" in a heartbreaking wail, endless as the
sobbing of the winter sea.

Till suddenly the door opened, and Janey came hurrying
in, bringing the candles and hot drinks; and as she drew the
heavy curtains, and plied the bellows to the fire, so that the
room gradually filled with golden, dancing light, he realized
that Red House was not all he had to lose, and that as long as
he had Janey, even if nought else, he would be happy.

So next year Red House was sold, and a spacious but
gloomy Georgian house taken, in Queen Square, Bloomsbury,
which would house both the family and the firm together.
Morris went for one last drive round the Red House country
before he tore himself away; then he never set eyes on it again,
lest his heart should break. And at midsummer they moved
to London.

Chapter 16

QUEEN SQUARE: THE CRAFTSMAN

Folk say a wizard to a northern king
At Christmas-tide such wondrous things did show,
That through one window men beheld the spring,
And through another saw the summer glow,
And through a third the fruited vines a-row,
While still, unheard, but in its wonted way,
Piped the drear wind of that December day.

So with this Earthly Paradise it is,
If ye will read aright, and pardon me,
Who strive to build a shadowy isle of bliss
Midmost the beating of the steely sea,
Where tossed about all hearts of men must be;
Whose ravening monsters mighty men shall slay,
Not the poor singer of an empty day.

The Earthly Paradise

WHAT a wretchedly dark November day it was! The fog was everywhere, creeping into Morris's very bones, even seeming to dull the large wood fire that burned in the room where he stood at work. For he was busy on one of those many designs which he printed on paper for walls, or on chintzes for curtains, covers, or wall-hangings, and which gave such a shock of delight to eyes accustomed to the stuffy red plush of the period, and were already making the firm famous. He sighed for Red House, as he had done a thousand times since he said good-bye to it and moved into Bloomsbury. Not that living in London had not its compensations. The journey from Upton every day and back, in the jolting, smoke-filled railway carriages, had been almost more than he could endure, and when he was quit of it he felt sometimes almost as if he could ' kiss the London pavements.' But, oh, the orchard-garden, which had been nearing perfection just as they had had to leave! And the irreplaceable freedom which one felt when in real country! For the thousandth time he groaned under the loss, and for the thousandth time sought relief by burying himself in his work.

And if anyone had the power to do so William Morris had, for he was gifted with as vivid an imagination as ever belonged to artist or poet. And, besides his pattern-designing, the rising firm gave him an ever-growing supply of the work that enthralled him. Indeed, he felt quite sure now that he had ' found himself' at last—not as a writer, architect, or painter, but in something which was a fusion of all three and more besides. For he was beginning to concern himself with every one of the things which make our homes beautiful, and the life we live in them healthy and enjoyable, in the very best senses. Indeed, later he was to go further still in his efforts to make the world beautiful and happy by throwing his vast energy into the battle to help the lot of the poorer classes, which was then beginning, and through which to-day so much is accomplished. Perhaps it would not be far wrong to call him a ' designer ' in the fullest sense of the word—a designer of life.

Another thing gained by the move to London was the leisure for writing poetry. True, he had written much on his journeys up and down from Upton, and had already planned to write something like a poetic version of all the best legends in the world; but, with the time he was now able to give to writing, this work of over forty-two thousand lines was done in the space of four years, and published under the title of *The Earthly Paradise*. It is perhaps the best known of his poetic works, and sets him among the great epic poets of all time. Full of rich imagery and vivid incident, beside it the *Æneid* itself seems drab and lifeless; and many a schoolboy must wish that the languages of these two might be reversed, and he have *The Earthly Paradise* to construe instead of Virgil; for, even if one is not very fond of poetry, this never fails to carry the mind away, as if by enchantment, to those glorious lands and times in which its twenty-four stories are set, and to show before each tale how the gliding seasons cast beauties before unnoted over our English countryside. And it never fails, too, to fill the most prosaic mind with a longing that the real world might be as it could be, if tilled and beautified by the labour and art of man, instead of being destroyed and despoiled by the foolish and wicked; for in such a real and ideal land the ancient stories are told. Morris searched through all the sources of legend for them—Medieval and Persian, Nordic and Greek—and he wrote or thought them out often while doing other work, and no doubt some of the romantic beauty of his designs is due to these poetic visions which filled his mind as he made them.

Later, when he took up weaving on the hand-loom, he used to find the rhythmic swing of the work no small stimulus to the writing of his Icelandic epic, *Sigurd the Volsung* (a poem based on the same legend as Wagner used for *The Ring*). For Morris had always looked upon poetry-writing as a pastime rather than a labour that needed hard concentration. And this gave to his work a unique naturalness and easy grace; and if his early poems make the heart ache, *The Earthly Paradise* comforts with its very earthly beauty, and to read it is like rambling, with Morris as companion, at leisure and with all worries forgotten, through a beautiful and unspoilt world on the loveliest of summer days.

In just such a ramble he was lost, that fog-bound November day, as the design, laid flat on the great table of pale scrubbed oak, was beginning to grow to his perfect satisfaction. A splendid pattern it was, based on the double peony, with the great crimson flowers fully open, and strong leaves asway in the wind; and all interwoven with the more delicate stems, intricate leaves, and subtly forked tendrils of the wild vine. The charcoal drawing finished, he was just dipping his brush in indian ink, to define the still hazily suggested outlines of flowers and leaves—after which the charcoal would be rubbed away with the spongy inside of the fresh loaf that stood ready— when he was brought sharply back to London and the November fog by the news that an " important customer " was waiting below.

So, combing his hair with charcoal-blackened fingers as he went downstairs, he prepared to face that part of the firm's work which was least to his taste. For the shining barouche which stood outside, with cockaded footman and tiger, both so stiff that they scarcely seemed alive, had brought one of the firm's richest admirers, Mrs Prinsep, of Little Holland House.

Though she had known Morris for some years, she can scarcely have believed that the rough-bearded person in the blue working blouse, with square, grimy hands, whose few words were growled out rather than spoken, was the actual creator of so many of the lovely things he proceeded to show her. Pattern delicate and poetic as had never before been seen, not even when Persian art flourished. Furniture simple, dignified, and delightfully lacking in those festoons of cabbage-like roses that were wont to smother most of the expensive furniture of the day, and painted with the pure, bright colours and unsophisticated beauty of a medieval illumination! Wine-glasses designed by Webb, beautiful in their severity, and dignified in their fitness for use. Embroideries designed by Rossetti or Morris, and sewn by Janey and her sister, or by Mrs Burne-Jones. Tiles for fireplaces, painted by all the friends together—even Charley Faulkner, even Swinburne, had tried their hands at it—and manufactured by William de Morgan, a new friend, who was later to revive the pottery arts of the Persians and Spanish Moors, and himself to equal or almost to surpass their work.

So many beautiful things, it was dazzling to the eyes of one who had long been a patron of artists and was herself a con-noisseur. She thrilled to think that here, in the midst of a century which she had begun to think hopelessly dead to art, was a scarcely yet opened mine of unprecedented genius! Why, the search for antiques was no longer necessary if one wished to furnish one's house with taste! And she would see that this genius was fully recognized, fully enabled to use itself to the utmost!

Such were the thoughts of Mrs Prinsep, the kindly and the rich, and such the thoughts of many another important person; so no wonder that the firm prospered, and soon gained com-missions for windows for cathedrals such as that at Oxford, and even for one of the drawing-rooms at Buckingham Palace! And thus the fortunes of Burne-Jones, Morris, and Rossetti became eventually secure, the demand for their work never waning or faltering as long as they lived.

The door of Queen Square was shut, away drove the shining barouche, and Morris was just about to return to his work, when his quick eye was caught by two faces in the square outside, which he thought he knew. Hesitating outside the house, they seemed about to come in, yet hung back uncertainly. No, he did not know them; yet he would have liked to, for they seemed fellow-lovers of beauty. They looked long at the window, then were about to move away, when a sudden impulse made Morris throw open the window.

"Come in," he cried, "if there's anything you'd like to see. You don't have to buy, you know!" he added encouragingly, as they came shyly back and mounted the steps.

"Well, I wish we could buy something, as we're just married, and are doing up our house, but we thought we couldn't really afford it, and ought to have machine-printed stuff."

Morris beamed inwardly. "You must be mistaken, sir," he said; "machine-printed stuff you ought *not* to have, for this will cost you *less*!"

And he began to show them pattern after pattern, eventually showering upon them more than they had ever expected to buy, yet at a price far below what they had expected to pay. They went out dazed, and Morris returned to his work with a rejoicing heart, for his patterns had gone for once to those who needed them—for whom he made them. "Oh, if only I could always afford it!" he sighed. "But the world will change one day! Then I shall work for *all* my fellow-men, not only for a few rich people; for all men need beauty; now only the few can buy it! Well, back to work!"

Soon he was drawing in the fine swinging lines, feeling the cool wind of June on the splendid, rain-heavy peonies, caressing with certain brush the strong yet tender shoots of the young vine; the fog, his visitors, and his prospects of future fame or wealth all equally forgotten.

Chapter 17

OXFORDSHIRE THAMES: THE POET

Forget six counties overhung with smoke,
Forget the snorting steam and piston stroke,
Forget the spreading of the hideous town;
Think rather of the pack-horse on the down,
The dream of London, small, and white, and clean,
The clear Thames bordered by its gardens green;
Think, that below bridge the green lapping waves
Smite some few keels that bear Levantine staves. . . .

The Earthly Paradise

HOW glad was Morris when the time for a holiday arrived, and he and Janey were able to forget London for a little! Since the loss of Red House he could never bear to go back to that part of the country, and of all the rest of the world that lay before him he loved Oxford best. Since childhood he had always liked a river, and the lowland meadows, and silver willows, aspens and alders, that make river land so lovely and tranquil, while the wandering of the stream leads your thoughts away!

So he took Janey and the girls to Oxford, and one of the poems in *The Earthly Paradise* recalls a day spent on the lonely and lovely Upper Thames. The meadows were at their best, and the river banks seemed like a changing tapestry as the boat glided by, so close and many-coloured grew their interwoven flowers.

Morris had pulled for an hour or more, and they had come to country utterly lonely and remote. Resting on his oars, he gazed around with eyes full of longing. Janey lay in the stern, no less beautiful than when he had first met her, but rather

94

more beautiful, so that he almost feared her. And to think that she must pass spring after spring, summer after summer, pent in by the grimy waste of sooty London! When he could afford it, very soon perhaps, he *would* live in the country, and somewhere like this it would be. He took out his notebook, and while the boat drifted slowly downstream, and the larks sang high up out of sight, he wrote:

> O June, O June, that we desired so,
> Wilt thou not make us happy on this day?
> Across the river thy soft breezes blow
> Sweet with the scent of beanfields far away,
> Above our heads rustle the aspens grey,
> Calm is the sky with harmless clouds beset,
> No thought of storm the morning vexes yet.

> See, we have left our hopes and fears behind
> To give our very hearts up unto thee;
> What better place than this then could we find
> By this sweet stream that knows not of the sea,
> That guesses not the city's misery,
> This little stream whose hamlets scarce have names,
> This far-off, lonely mother of the Thames?

"That's for *The Earthly Paradise*," he said, as Janey looked up from her work of embroidery; then he took up the oars and rowed another mile, feeling all the happier for having done something to earn his holiday.

Another day they went with a party of friends down the river to Dorchester, where the abbey stands among thick willows and a network of waterways, close by the flood-lands of the river. Leaving their boat, they walked up to the great down, with its crown of beeches and encircling, turf-grown mound, left there by some Roman army, camping there long ago. It was hot climbing the hill, and the sun beat mercilessly on back and head, and all were glad when they reached the crest and a light west wind came to cool them. Morris, who was never tired, cheered the others on, and was the first to climb the steep, turfy wall, and to reach the cool shades of the beeches. After the dazzling sun outside, the shade was so deep the very air seemed green, as if beneath the sea. The whispering winds ran sweetly through the boughs, and the doves sang without ceasing in the deep jade canopy high above them, as the party lay down to cool themselves; and Morris, opening the great basket which he had carried so easily up the hill, began to spread one of the splendid teas to which he loved to treat his friends (not forgetting his own teacup, which held a good pot of tea, "for then," he would say to Janey, "when you've poured it out you needn't worry about me any more").

What a perfect day it was, and how perfectly they spent it! If only all such days were spent so—not just holidays, but all days—for why should work mean ugly and squalid surround, ings? Why, in a little town like Dorchester, lying there below them, how lovely life could be, how lovely it must have been for those who built the church down there—country people, no doubt, not contractors from London, as they would be nowadays! And, though simple people, what masters of beauty! Their buildings could never be equalled now, not even by skilled artists, for they had the simple loveliness that comes only of a simple life in lovely surroundings. "And thus must *I* live," said Morris to himself, "if I am to create things equal to theirs. And thus I *shall* live."

So Morris thought, and between talk and thought the after, noon glided away, till the sun lost its blazing strength, and the whispering of leaves ceased as the calm of dusk came on; and the friends walked down again to Dorchester, and rowed back to Oxford under a primrose evening sky, all tired, pensive, happy in the perfect day, yet sad that it was over.

In Morris the sadness became a strange exasperation, when he thought how many were the days no less lovely that were wasted by men as if they had no value. And, indeed, to most men they did seem to have less value than money or power. Yet this was surely because there was something wrong with the world—because all was strife and competition, instead of unity and fellowship; riches and poverty, instead of general well-being? Well, he would do what he could to change things; and if he failed—no matter, he would have had the joy of the work and the hope that it would bring him, and after all, without something to work and hope for, what was life worth? Work was joy, or should be, if only all men could choose, as he had done, the work they liked and were best at!

The stars had begun to twinkle as he took out his notebook, and he could scarcely see to write the poem which afterwards went into *The Earthly Paradise*, and which preserves the evening on the hill-top so perfectly that it seems but yesterday to us, though sheep-bells have never rung there for over fifty years!

Across the gap made by our English hinds,
Amidst the Roman's handiwork, behold
Far off the long-roofed church; the shepherd binds
The withy round the hurdles of his fold,
Down in the foss the river fed of old,
That through long lapse of time has grown to be
The little grassy valley that you see.

Rest here awhile, not yet the eve is still,
The bees are wandering yet, and you may hear
The barley mowers on the trenched hill,
The sheep-bells and the restless changing weir,
All little sounds made musical and clear
Beneath the sky that burning August gives,
While yet the thought of glorious Summer lives.

Chapter 18

THE EARTHLY PARADISE FOUND

I have been looking for a house for the wife and kids, and whither do you guess my eye is turned now? Kelmscott, a little village about two miles above Radcott Bridge—a heaven on earth; an old stone Elizabethan house like Water Eaton, and such a garden! close down on the river, a boat house and all things handy.

MORRIS, *in a letter to Faulkner, May 17, 1871*

WHEN Morris moved to London he had sought relief by burying himself in his creative work, but he could never truly resign himself to the loss of the beauty and freedom of the country, which had meant so much to him all his life. Indeed, the ugliness of London oppressed him more and more, and by the time he had spent five years there, five years of precious life and youth, he felt he could bear it no longer. For London, though smaller than now, was far more squalid and dirty; and the conditions of the poor of those days astonish one now, so great has the change been since then. In those days hunger was a common thing among the poor, and bare-footed children in winter were no rare sight. As for housing, it was appalling beyond belief. Reform, it is true, had begun. Ruskin had been in the field since Morris was at Oxford, and the Prince Consort had made untiring efforts to improve the conditions of the poor; but as yet the face of things was little better than twenty years before, in those terrible years the ' hungry forties.'

And this exasperation at the waste, not of his own life only, but of that of numberless other people, is felt ever and again between the stories in *The Earthly Paradise*. " Time passes, Youth passes, Age and Death will soon be upon us," is expressed over and over. Most beautifully in such a refrain as,

> Kiss me, Love, for who knoweth
> What thing cometh after Death?

most explicitly in,

> Thus do we work that thou mayest take away!
> Look at this beauty of young children's mirth,
> Soon to be swallowed by thy noiseless dearth!
> Look at this faithful love that knows no end
> Unless thy cold thrill through it thou shouldst send!
> Look at this hand ripening to perfect skill,
> Unless the fated measure thou shouldst fill!
> This eager knowledge that would stop for nought,
> Unless thy net both chase and hunter caught!

It was partly this exasperation, and discontent with all his own surroundings, that led Morris to the study of Icelandic, and soon to go to Iceland. For of all civilized countries Iceland had kept longest its form of government and system of laws, which were said to have changed little since the fifteenth century. This and some knowledge of the epics in which Icelandic literature abounds must have attracted Morris strongly; especially as those epics, unlike those of Greece and Rome, were little known and quite unhackneyed. So he set himself to learn Icelandic, and with the help of Mr Magnusson, his teacher, began to translate the sagas, and soon to publish his translations.

And if anyone was suited to translate them Morris was; for they are rich beyond all other epics in the warrior exploits which appealed so much to his boyish heart, as they are in the atmosphere of the free, wild, untilled earth before man mastered it, which must have attracted so much the artist in him, in his conscious revolt against the civilized ugliness of his time.

The journey to Iceland, when decided upon, was looked forward to with all the eagerness of a schoolboy anticipating the perfect holiday; for much of the island was uninhabited, and to travel about it, as he meant to do, one must go on horseback, carrying one's own food and camping things.

Charley Faulkner was prevailed upon to come, and a new acquaintance, Mr Evans, who was anxious to see Iceland, took the opportunity of going in their company. Mr Magnusson made a fourth and, as an Icelander, very valuable member of the party.

They were to leave Granton harbour on July the 9th, and to be away about six weeks. Meanwhile a cavalcade of twenty-five or thirty horses was being collected at Reykjavik, where the party was to land and start inland. Money was sent out, and a hundred other preparations were made.

No wonder it was eagerly looked forward to, and all the more happily because in the spring of that year Morris had gained one of the greatest blessings of his life. In searching for somewhere for Janey and the girls to go to for their summer holiday, he found the house on the Upper Thames which fulfilled so much all the longings of the last five years—consoling him at last for what he had thought must hurt him all his life, the loss of Red House—that it seemed to him nothing less than his own Earthly Paradise come true.

He saw the house in an advertisement by chance, and, though he had little hope of its being suitable—for it was a manor house, and he was really looking for something much smaller—something made him take the journey to see it—not least, perhaps, its situation in that very country of the Upper Thames where he had rowed with Janey and the children four years before, and which he had left with such an aching heart!

So off he went. In his suit of dark blue pilot cloth and blue, home-dyed cotton shirt—for he had long discarded the stiff collar and tie of the period—his soft felt hat, oak stick, and satchel, with his lunch and some work for the journey, he must have looked something like a pilgrim, something like a shepherd. A friend once compared him to Christian in *Pilgrim's Progress*.

How sweet was the spring air as he got down from the train at last, and mounted the trap that was waiting to take him to the remote hamlet where the house lay! As they trotted through the fair country the swallows circled around them, and a fresh wind set the green corn-lands waving and whispering. Far away southward he could see the line of silver blue which he knew for the White Horse Hills, where Marlborough and Avebury lay. And as far away northward another line, silver-blue likewise, showed where the first slopes of the Cotswolds began. Eastward, behind him, in the midst of that wide plain of the Upper Thames, rose Faringdon Folly, with its well-known circle of firs. How often he had looked up to it from the river! Why, he thought he had explored all this country; yet Kelmscott, whither the pony was steadily trotting, was a name he had never before heard. Perhaps it was too small a place to be marked on an ordinary map? Well, so much the better if it was! Certainly it was strangely remote, farther from this noisy, ugly century than he had dared to hope. League on league the cornfields lay so sweetly green, so gently caressed by the wind, and with no end that he could see, except those silver-blue barriers north and south, between which ran the wandering river, with its blue and silver waves, towards Oxford, London, and the sea.

On trotted the pony for six or seven miles, till at last, beneath a ponderous group of giant elms, a small grey bell-cot showed, and soon he heard its bells, sounding thinly and clearly above the faint crowing of the cocks and gentle lowing of the cattle.

Then came a high and crumbling wall, of grey stone gilded with lichen, and crested with wallflowers and tall white camomile daisies. A fig-tree showing over it and the high summits of well-clipped yews, and beyond them a glimpse of silver stone gables and chimneys, and the scent, so utterly sweet, of garden flowers told him their journey was done.

Morris sent away the trap, and stood for some minutes inhaling the lovely scent and listening to the loud calling of the blackbirds; the beauty was so dreamlike, there among the cornfields under the elms! His heart almost stopped beating as he touched the old blue door in the wall and lifted its heavy ring. Hope and fear played with him as they had never done since that summer afternoon thirteen years before, when the thunder-shower beat down the scarlet lilies, in that long, narrow garden of Holywell. Yet it was hope mostly, for the old house seemed to be drawing him in.

How thick the flowers were as he entered! The may was like white foam, and the scent of early honeysuckle filled the air. Saffron butterflies were lazily floating in the slant sun, above the starry lauristinus, and all his tiredness fell away like a forgotten dream. Though no one answered his knock, after some time he entered, for windows and doors were open to the fragrant, sun-cured air, and he wandered freely about the empty rooms. No soul was there, but it seemed full of a strange friendliness and beauty which he had always desired. Quiet light streamed through the leaded windows, with their curious glass, and lay in each old room like a blessing; and down the sunny paths, and beyond a little meadow, the river ran silverly by. A still, dark, and lovely brook made an island, where chestnut and willow branches waved up and down, like some tapestry in a dream.

Wandering into the garden, Morris found a bowed old

man in a straw hat, who looked up as his shoulder was touched, and pulled at his forelock.

" I have taken this house," Morris said. " Where can I find the owner to tell him?"

" Mr Hobbs? He was here just a while ago. He'll likely be over the wall there, along with his bulls." Morris followed his glance to where the tall barn gable, pigeon-tower, and some yellow rick-tops showed beyond the garden trees, and, thanking the gardener, went swiftly towards them. After a search he found the bull-house, and in it a tall man in green coat, white beaver hat, and large gold albert, with whom he arranged to rent the house from year to year. Then he walked back to the tiny village cross, where the trap was to wait for him.

Morris felt the wonder of his discovery so deeply that he was neither gay nor sad, but only solemn, as he journeyed home. Since the house was larger than he needed or could easily afford, he decided to ask Rossetti to share it with him, which he gladly agreed to do; and that summer, with Janey and the girls at Kelmscott, Rossetti spent perhaps the happiest months of his life.

Chapter 19

JOURNEY TO ICELAND

Yet he durst not raise his eyes awhile and look on the land, lest
he should see Death manifest therein. At last he looked, and
saw that he was high up amongst the mountain-peaks: before
him and on either hand was but a world of fallow stone rising
ridge upon ridge like the waves of the wildest of the winter sea.
The sun not far from its midmost shone down bright and hot on
that wilderness; yet there was no sign that any man had ever been
there since the beginning of the world.

The Land of the Glittering Plain

AS the night train to Granton roared northward at a
good fifty-five the rain rattled on the panes, and clung
in little quivering drops that glittered in the dim lamp-
light from the railway carriage.

"But you really ought to sleep, you know, Top," said a
voice behind Morris, who was pacing up and down the
corridor, hoping for some hint of the dawning of the day
upon which he was to set sail for Iceland. It was the third
time Faulkner had tried to get him to rest, but his excitement,
he knew, was too great.

"Thanks, Charley, but I can't. Don't you worry," he said,
and Faulkner's tired, anxious face disappeared once more into
the carriage. Not that he felt he could sleep either, for the
strong cigars which Mr Evans smoked continually were almost
more than his stomach could stand. So he got out his note-
books and began to check his calculations, for, as a mathe-
matical scholar, the finance and timetable work of the party
had, of course, been assigned to him.

In the other corner Magnusson, who never seemed tired,

was chatting gaily with a commercial traveller, with whom he was sharing a flask of brandy, and a knowledge of Iceland, and discussing with painful detail the national fare, which both seemed to relish, though their descriptions only made Faulkner feel worse. Avoiding them with his eyes, he looked across at Mr Evans, and wondered what sort of fellow-traveller he was going to prove. The hair and whiskers so well oiled and brushed, the smoking-cap of red morocco, the polished boots poised together on the foot-warmer, the solid pigskin luggage and gun-cases that filled the rack above him! He was wondering how he and Topsy would get on, when Evans cast down the book he was reading and looked up. " A queer chap, Ruskin!" he exclaimed. " I've never tried to read him before, and now I'm damned if I know what he means!" Faulkner longed to explain, and defend the man who was such a hero to Morris and himself—but no, not a word; all tact would be needed if Topsy and Evans were to get on smoothly, and he must do his best to see that they did.

Just then Morris looked in. " It's day!" he shouted. " Come on—wake up, Charley!"

Charley looked out, but he could see only the furnace fires of the factories glowing on the horizon; it was not the dawn—not for two hours yet. He told Morris, who strode back to his vigil, looking rather angry and not a trifle tired.

" What a giant of strength he is!" thought Faulkner, as he nodded in a half-sleep. If only I had some of it! Why, I've followed other men all my life, while he's led them! Yet one can't change one's nature, and who's more worth following than Topsy! Without him what would I be! Why, I owe him all that's made my life worth while. So never mind; I'll be his disciple gladly while I have strength, though hard it is sometimes!"

And harder yet it was to be in future years, though Faulkner never ceased to follow Topsy, into politics as he had into art and literature, till his delicate constitution failed, and he died when scarcely middle-aged.

He was asleep, when in rushed Morris again, and as he opened the carriage door in rushed a flood of brilliant light from the great red rising sun.

Soon after daybreak—July the 8th, '71—the travellers left Granton harbour for Iceland. Their ship, the *Diana*, was a little wooden paddle-steamer of 240 tons, working under both sail and steam, and she rolled considerably as they met the fresh wind and waves of the open sea. Morris stood on deck most of the day, his head teeming with visions of the legendary country he was soon to see in reality. For nights past his impatience had hardly let him or his friends sleep, but now that his adventures could be looked upon as already begun he seemed calmer, and full of boyish happiness.

They had left Granton on Sunday, and early on Tuesday the Faroes were in sight. He wrote in his diary:

> I confess I shuddered at my first sight of a really northern land in the grey of a coldish morning. (The Faroes seemed to me such a gentle, sweet place when we saw them again after Iceland.) The hills were not high, especially on one side, as they slope beachless into the clear but grey water; the grass was grey between greyer ledges of stone that divided the hills in regular steps; it was not savage, but mournfully empty and barren, the grey clouds, dragging over the hill-tops or lying in the hollows, being the only thing that varied the grass, stone, and sea: yet as we went on, the firth opened out on one side and showed wild, strange hills and narrow sounds between the islands, that had something, I don't know what, of poetic and attrac-tive about them; and on one side was sign of population in the patches of bright green that showed the homefields of farms on the hillsides, and at last at the bight's end we saw the pleasant-looking little town of Thorshaven, with its green-roofed little houses cluster-ing round a little bay and up a green hill-side: thereby we presently cast anchor. The shore soon became excited at our arrival, and boats put off to us, and there was a great deal of kissing on deck presently: then came a smart looking boat carrying the governor, and having

eight oars aside, manned by the queerest old carles, who by way of salute as the boat touched our side, shuffled off their Faroish caps in a very undignified manner.

They landed to walk across the island.

Presently, having gone through the town, we met on a road that ran through little fields nearly ready for the scythe: it affected me strangely to see all the familiar flowers growing in a place so different to anything one had ever imagined, and withal (it had grown a very bright day by now) there was real beauty about the place of a kind I can't describe. We were soon off these cultivated meadows however, in a long deep valley of the open fells, peaty and grass-clad, with a small stream running through it, and not unlike to many Cumberland valleys I have been in: up the hillside on the left we struck, and clomb the hill, whence turning round, we could see the sound we had come up this morning, the little *Diana* lying in harbour with boats clustered round her, the little toy-like town so small, so small, and beyond it the mountains, jagged and peaked, of another island, with the added interest of knowing that there was a deep sound between us and them: sea and sky were deep blue now, but the white clouds yet clung to the mountains here and there.

After dinner they re-embarked, and all the evening the *Diana* was threading the long, narrow sound between towering cliffs; until at last they reached the gates that were to lead them again into the open sea.

. . . narrow enough they look even now we are quite near; as the ship's nose was almost in them, I saw close beside us a stead with its homefield sloping down to the sea, the people running out to look at us, and the black cattle grazing all about; then I turned to look ahead as the ship met the first swell in the open sea, and when I looked astern a very few minutes later I could see nothing at all of the gates we had come out by, no slopes of grass, or valleys opening out from the shore; nothing but a terrible wall of rent and furrowed rocks, the little clouds still entangled here and there about the tops of them: there was no beach below the wall, no foam breaking at its feet; it was midnight now and everything was grey, and colourless, and shadowless, yet there was light enough in the clear air to see every cranny and nook of the rocks, and in the north-east now the grey sky began to get a little lighter with dawn.

Two days afterwards they sighted Iceland, and, running beneath its dark mountains to Reykjavik, they landed. During the next two days the final preparations were made, and on Monday, July the 17th, with two guides and about thirty horses, the expedition set out.

That evening

> we came into a soft grassy meadow bordered by a little stream, and jumped off our horses after a ride of six hours and a half: it was a cold night, though clear and fine, and we fell hard to unpack the tents and pitch them while the guides unburdened the horses, who were soon rolling about in every direction, and then set to work diligently to feed: the tents being pitched, Magnusson and Faulkner set to work to light the fire, while Evans and I went about looking for game, about the hill spurs and the little tarn between the lava and our camp: it was light enough to see to read; wonderfully clear, but not like daylight, for there were no shadows at all: I turned back often from the slopes to look down on the little camp, and the grey smoke that now began to rise up, and felt an excitement and pleasure not easy to express: till I had to get to my shooting, which I didn't like at all: however, I shot two golden plovers and came back to camp with them.

Thus the travellers went northward across the island. Everywhere the barrenness and great loneliness, and the pitiless icefields that showed above and beyond their giant clefts, impressed Morris more than he could say in words. Once they passed close to a glacier, and dismounted to clamber about it. Morris slipped and nearly broke his neck, but this seemed a small thing in all the day's work.

At the Geysirs poor Faulkner was ill, and they had to remain still for a day or two, while storm-winds swept by and pitiless rain poured down. Morris felt impatient, for he despised the Geysirs as a sight attractive to tourists and scientists, but not to seekers after the magic and beauty of legendary days! Yet some impression they had on him nevertheless: "near our camp," said Mr Evans afterwards, "there were several pools of beautiful, still, blue, boiling water: it was in these holes we boiled our fish, and fetched our hot water: but after we had each been several times, Morris on returning from one of these expeditions said it was so uncanny he could not go again."

Leaving the Geysirs, they went on northward towards the sea. The bitter wind against them, and often rain too, rising sometimes almost to a blizzard, made the crossing of this bleak wilderness a severe trial to every one's temper. Yet they held out somehow, Morris not least, for on this six days' ride they passed several places of epic fame—the cavern of Surts-hellir, Erne-water-heath, and Erne-water, "a most mournful desolate-looking place with no signs of life as we rode up but for a swan that rose trumpeting from the lakeside."

And many another place, made famous in old legend, they saw. Now and then the change between Iceland of the past and present affected Morris deeply:

. . . just think, though, what a mournful place this is—Iceland, I mean—setting aside the pleasure of one's animal life there, the fresh air, the riding and the rough life, and feeling of adventure; —how every place and name marks the death of its short-lived eager-ness and glory: and withal so little is the life changed in some ways: Olaf Peacock went about summer and winter after his live-stock, and saw to his hay-making and fishing, just as this peak-nosed parson does. I don't doubt the house stands on the old ground. —But Lord! what littleness and helplessness has taken the place of the old passion and violence that had place here once! Set aside the hope that the unseen sea gives you here, and the strange threatening change of the blue spiky mountains beyond the firth, and the rest seems emptiness and nothing else; a piece of turf under your feet, and the sky overhead, that's all: whatever solace your life is to have here must come out of yourself or these old stories, not over hopeful themselves.

In Broadfirth they found a ship bound for England, and he had a chance to send a hurried note home:

Give dear love to the little ones, and tell them I am going to try and bring them my pretty grey pony home. His name is Falcon, and when he is in good condition he ambles beautifully, fast and deliciously soft. I wish you could see us to understand how jolly it is when we have got a good piece of road, and the whole train of twenty-eight horses is going a good round trot, the tin cups tinkling, and the boxes rattling. Goodbye, my dear, I have so often thought of the sweet, fresh garden at Kelmscott, and you and the little ones in it, and wished you happy.

Falcon, however, fell lame, and it was Mouse instead who was brought back to Kelmscott, and lived there, much beloved by the family for long and happy years.

The last place of importance to be seen was the richest of all in association, both historical and legendary—the place where every year, in heroic times, the laws of Iceland had been proclaimed. It was a little grassy hill at the base of a towering mountain wall, girt on all sides by narrow but deep clefts down which a torrent rushed, and on the hill was the mound on which the warrior chieftains sat. Not a builded stone was there, for it was a place made almost impregnable by nature from attack, a little mound of flowery turf only; yet it must have been the most solemn and awe-inspiring place in the old days; and so no less it was to Morris, as he stood there trying to picture in his mind the scenes of epic times: the warriors in all their war-gear, their splendid flowing beards and rugged, grand, fierce features; and their chieftains more splendid still. How he would have loved just a sight of it!

From imagination he woke to the Iceland of the nineteenth century, with its mean-featured, spiritless folk. What had happened? Had the influence of the civilized world swept over Iceland too, making everything prosaic which had once been epic? Perhaps it had, and things would remain so till civilization should change, and become what it should be at last— like the old days in so far as those days were noble and beautiful, unlike them in so far as they were cruel and unjust and ugly. Such was the life of the land he had long sought, but was realizing more and more that he would never find—not even here in this remote island. Nowhere but in the doubtful future, which he would never see. Well, if he was not to see it, he could at least help to bring it about. Let this be his aim, and the reward, he knew, would not fail to be his—the reward of having used one's talent for the helping of one's fellows—for thus only can any true talent be fulfilled, and the sense of that fulfilment is the only reward in life worth seeking.

The ride back to Reykjavik was short and swift, the horses knowing well that they were going home. The travellers boarded the *Diana* laden with presents for home, not least among them being the fat little grey pony. On September the 6th they sailed into Granton, and a few days later Morris was at Kelmscott.

Chapter 20

ROSSETTI PAINTING AT
KELMSCOTT

Conjuga clara poeta et præclarissima vultu
Denique pictura clara sit illa mea!
ROSSETTI, *inscribed on Mrs Morris's portrait*

WHILE Morris was in Iceland the English summer
had grown lovelier day by day. The garden at
Kelmscott, being close to the river, was so fertile
that lilies and roses, that elsewhere have to be pampered, grew
there almost of themselves; while the mown grass under the
apple-trees was a carpet of the softest emerald. Here Rossetti
would sit, talking to Janey, or silently, while she embroidered
and he wrote or painted. Often their meals were served to
them among the lily-beds under the great mulberry-tree, into
which May and Jenny used to climb to rescue the ruby fruits
from the blackbirds, who banqueted there summer-long.

Sometimes they took long walks, through the flowering river-meadows towards Lechlade, or up the hill towards the shades of Lord Faringdon's woods, whence, looking back northward, you could see all the plain between there and the Cotswolds, and here and there a glimpse of the blue river winding away towards the Wytham and Cumnor hills.

Rossetti did many drawings of Janey, lying at ease on the sofa or sitting sewing in the garden; and he finished a great oil painting of her, begun some years before, and meant as a wedding present to her and William. In it she sits gazing dreamily away, in a silk dress of deep peacock blue, a crystal heart on her necklace. Before her, in one of Webb's tall glasses, are white roses, and tendrils of the vine growing outside the window. The picture might almost be an illustration to Morris's early poem *Beata Mea Domina*.

It was one of the earliest of those many paintings which Rossetti did from her, from life or from memory, and the haunting beauty and intense sadness of these pictures have suggested many legends about him and her. The best-known story is, of course, the most romantic one—that they were lovers; but to anyone who knows anything about her demure, religious nature this is obviously impossible. It is also some-times said that Rossetti loved Janey, without his love being returned; this may well be true, and there is no shame in it, but even for this theory there is little evidence beyond the fact that he painted her so often, and joined with every one else who knew her in admiring a haunting beauty, remembered with tear-filled eyes by some alive to this day. Certainly, had there been anything serious between them, Morris, who adored Janey all his life, and was no fool, would never have left them alone together when he went to Iceland. And, though he broke his joint tenancy with Rossetti some years later, it is known to be due to their complete incompatibility as house-mates, not to any question of jealousy over Janey. And the same applies to their final estrangement, slightly later, over the affairs of the firm; for, though Rossetti was never the drug-sodden wreck he is sometimes held to be, he was as much a lover of Bohemian town life as Morris was of the simple life of the country, and the wonder is not in their separation, but in the fact that they remained close friends so long. Indeed, out of the tangle of stories and scandal that is woven round Rossetti the one lasting impression is of intensest pity for the loneliness of his life—whether by his own fault or not, a life which shows in strongest contrast to that of Morris, who was one of the most fortunate artists ever born. And perhaps this comparison did occur to Rossetti, and increase the bitterness which finally parted them.

Besides drawing and painting Janey, Rossetti also did chalk portraits of Jenny and May—and two of his loveliest drawings these certainly are. They hang side by side at Kelmscott to this day, as does the portrait of Janey, in the white panelled room where they were done. They took long, for Rossetti was slow and careful, and always put deep thought into his work. But he was no less kind and generous, and did his best to amuse his sitters, and when the work was done he gave to each a little gold watch as a reward, for his gifts were always princely.

What a perfect summer it was! Between working in the garden, gliding down the river, and walking in the country the days passed like a dream. The only sad thing was Morris's absence, and the lack of the zest and jollity that he always gave to any company of friends he was in. And, since he could not post letters, Janey sometimes felt unbearably anxious about him, and was very glad of Gabriel's urbane and friendly presence. When at last news did arrive the relief was immeasurable, and anxiety gave place to looking forward to seeing him again and to hearing about his adventures.

At last he returned, looking more rough and Viking-like than ever. Rossetti's pictures of Janey and the girls seemed to him some of the loveliest portraits he had ever seen, and he felt he had never admired Gabriel's work so much before.

And he, though he had been impelled to make his journey by a true craving of the soul, now that that need was satisfied, felt infinitely happy to be home. After the chill remoteness and lifeless loneliness of the plains and creeks and gorges of Iceland, Kelmscott seemed a Paradise of fruit and flowers, like the Garden of Pomona, or the Isles of the Blest!

How he loved the *life* of it! How he loved the seasons and the changes of the year! This garden close, glowing with autumnal fruit, as it had glowed, last time he saw it, with early summer flowers! And his good luck made him immeasurably glad.

" Truly," he told himself, as he sat with Janey and Gabriel beneath the mulberry-tree, watching the swaying of the great tiger-lilies, and listening to the hum of the bees, and children's voices playing somewhere beyond the rose-hedge, where the orchard trees were ponderous with gold and russet fruit, " truly," he told himself over and over, " this *is*, this *is* the Earthly Paradise."

Chapter 21

LOVE IS ENOUGH

I went on working, famous now, with many who almost wor-
shipped me, for the words I had said, the many things I had
taught them; and I in return verily loved these earnestly.

Early Romances

MORRIS returned to his illuminating with new
pleasure, and also to writing. By the end of the year
a new composition was fairly finished—to his complete
dissatisfaction, however. So in February he went down alone
to Kelmscott, and wrestled fiercely with the work for two weeks.
When he departed it was to carry away the perfected form of
Love is Enough, a medieval morality poem of most exquisite
beauty and intricacy, which cost him more trouble than any
other poem he wrote.

If love be real, if I whom ye behold
Be ought but glittering wings and gown of gold,
Be ought but singing of an ancient song
Made sweet by record of dead stingless wrong,
How shall we part at that sad garden's end
Through which the ghosts of mighty lovers wend?

. . . . . .

Love is enough: though the world be a-waning
And the woods have no voice but the voice of complaining,
Though the skies be too dark for dim eyes to discover
The gold-cups and daisies fair blooming thereunder,
Though the hills be held shadows and the sea a dark wonder,
And this day draw a veil over all deeds passed over,
Yet their hands shall not tremble, their feet shall not falter,
The void shall not weary, the fear shall not alter
These lips and these eyes of the loved and the lover.

. . . . . .

Love is enough: while ye deemed him a-sleeping,
 There were signs of his coming and sounds of his feet;
His touch it was that would bring you to weeping,
 When the summer was deepest and music most sweet:
In his footsteps ye followed the day to its dying,
Ye went forth by his gown-skirts the morning to meet:
 In his place on the beaten-down orchard-grass lying,
 Of the sweet ways ye pondered yet left for life's trying.
  . . . .

Come—pain ye shall have, and be blind to the ending!
Come—fear ye shall have, mid the sky's overcasting!
Come—change ye shall have, for far are ye wending!
Come—no crown ye shall have for your thirst and your fasting!
But the kissed lips of Love and fair life everlasting!

Thus sounds the heart-touching music of it. Read through
but once in a lifetime, it will haunt the mind for ever.

The celebration of his birthday, on March the 24th, though
planned so joyfully by the children, once again filled him, as
it had for many years now, with gloomsome thoughts. Thirty-
eight he was this time, so they told him. *Already* thirty-eight!
And really so little done—and so much, so much, to do! To
crowd into the numbered, ebbing hours! Better to have had
only one means of self-expression—then he remembered the
boy of fourteen, restless night and day for lack of any, and he
was thankful for things being as they were.

Besides the painted books he was making, there was always
much work for the firm—bread-and-cheese work, as he called
it. Design followed design, with scarcely a glance back, the
last touch laid.

The next spring brought a pleasant interlude, a journey
with Burne-Jones to Italy. To the occupant of the Grange,
Hammersmith, it was a heavenly interlude, but Morris was
not willing to let himself be much pleased with anything,
though twice earth's beauty took him out of his ill humours
unawares. The descent to Turin, through a land of verdure
and blossoms and snow-capped mountains, and the impressive
glories of the Apennines, filled him with the wonder and

pleasure he should have felt for Italian architecture and art, but did not.

So after a short stay he came back to England alone, and began arrangements—together with the faithful Faulkner—for another journey, this time with all his heart. It was their second and last pilgrimage to Iceland, and this time they went farther inland, and were lost to the world for over two months amid those Northern wastes.

His estrangement from Rossetti, and the fact that he still held a partnership in the firm, caused Morris no little business worry; for, though Rossetti and several others had been partners in the creation of the firm, the only one who had given it his regular attention was Morris himself, and it was through his hard, regular work, during ten years and more, that it had become securely established, and it was on it that he and his family chiefly depended now for a living. All the same, each of the others, who had helped to put up the trifling amount of capital on which the firm started, was legally entitled to claim a share of what it had now become worth—a position which gave Morris much anxiety, when in '74 the partnership was, at his request, dissolved, and the firm became simply Morris and Co.

Of the six partners, Burne-Jones, Faulkner, and Webb refused to claim anything; but Rossetti, Madox Brown, and Marshall claimed their full share. Of Marshall we know little. He probably looked on the affair as on any other financial speculation that had turned out well, and saw no reason for refraining from claiming what his luck had won for him.

Madox Brown, we know, was poor, and, besides this, though he had done little direct work to help the firm, he may well have felt that, as one of the earliest pioneers of the artistic movement in which the younger men had made their fortunes, but by which he himself had been so unjustly neglected, he was only helping himself to some of the share of the prosperity that should by rights have been his. For Morris had been

Rossetti's disciple, and Rossetti had been Madox Brown's, and had taken endless kindnesses from him, even money which he could ill afford, yet had given ungrudgingly.

And in the same way Rossetti felt that, if not directly, he was indirectly and considerably to be thanked for the success which Morris had been able to achieve. Indeed, without the hard and often thankless work of those early pioneers the Pre-Raphaelites and their champion, Ruskin, whose giant struggles drove more artistic conscience into the British public than it ever felt before or has shown since, the art of Morris and Burne-Jones must have fallen on barren soil, and their lot have been poverty and neglect. But as it was they were born into what can justly be called the Golden Age of art in England.

Anyhow, whatever the private reasons of Rossetti and Madox Brown may have been, their action must certainly have been in some way justifiable, for both were honourable and generous-hearted to a high degree, and, though Morris was never reconciled to Rossetti, his coolness with Brown was eventually made up.

Nor, indeed, was the refusal of Burne-Jones and Webb to take anything as quixotic as it at first seems, for, though not directly to the firm, to Morris indirectly their debt was exceedingly great. And to both their friendship with him, and the help his comparative wealth had enabled him to give them, had been of immense value. Through Morris, Burne-Jones had got the commissions for church decorations which had helped him so much at first, besides many commissions from Morris himself—the decorations at Red House, for instance—for which he was paid most generously; while the commission for the design of Red House itself, coming to Webb at the very beginning of his career as an architect, gave him a very good start, besides leading to the building of " Clouds." [1]

---

[1] A large country mansion in Wiltshire, Webb's masterpiece.

Chapter 22

HAMMERSMITH: DAWN OF SOCIALISM

This land we have loved in our love and our leisure
    For them hangs in Heaven, high out of their reach;
The wide hills o'er the sea-plain for them have no pleasure,
    The grey homes of their fathers no story to teach.

The singers have sung and the builders have builded,
    The painters have fashioned their tales of delight;
For what and for whom hath the world's book been gilded,
    When all is for these but the blackness of night?

The Message of the March Wind

WITH these worries off his mind, and the firm really his own, Morris at once began to use his freedom by plunging into one new activity after another, so that the firm grew steadily, till Queen Square could house it no longer. Already Janey and the children had had to give up their part of the house, and move to a small place at Turnham Green—all that could be found at the time. There they had to remain for several years, consoled only by the precious holiday visits to Kelmscott, until at last Morris found the spacious Georgian house by the river at Hammersmith, with the large, rambling garden behind, which finally became their London home. With this and Kelmscott, and the firm ever flourishing and growing, it would seem that all Morris could desire was achieved, his life a golden dream of beauty and beauty's creation, all things, for him and those he loved most, at their utter best; but two years before they found this home on the Upper Mall a tragedy that was to sadden all future joys had fallen into their happy circle. Jenny, aged just sixteen, whose brilliant intellect had been an ever-growing delight to her father, and to whom he was beginning to be able to talk about the things of the mind which he valued most—art and literature and the world's beauty—as to no one else he had ever known, was suddenly seized by epilepsy, and soon all hopes of any bright future were over. Few can imagine the sadness of such a thing: her budding life ruined, her mind and beauty useless, and her father filled with more pain and regret than he would ever confess, even to himself. Coming at first only in occasional fits, as years went by it gained so upon her that she had to be temporarily and then permanently secluded in the home in which, as late as 1935, her tragic life closed.

In October of '78, though, when the Morrises went to live at Hammersmith, re-christening their new home Kelmscott House, hope for her recovery was far from given up, and Jenny and May must have rejoiced in their new home no less than did William and Janey. The river was so close—only separated from their front door by the width of a small road grown with lofty trees, so that their south windows looked through the changing design of leaves and branches straight over the wide waters, which on sunny days cast a network of rainbow lights up on to the ceilings, as the little waves, that had not so long before passed through the flowered meadows of Kelmscott itself, flowed sparkling by.

Not long after they moved in Morris had a loom set up in his bedroom. The firm had started brocade-weaving some time ago—shuttle-weaving, that is, with a repeating pattern, like those which on his chintzes were printed with inked wood blocks. The success which he had gained urged Morris to try the most ambitious thing of all, the weaving of tapestry, in which each stitch is laid by hand, like the brush-strokes on a painting. With the craftsman's conscientious thoroughness which had saved him again and again from the failures that so often overtake artists who are not craftsmen, he began by learning to weave himself, from the very beginning. As his time was more than full already he had to *make* time, and did so by rising even earlier than his wont, and often putting in several hours at his tapestry work before the rest of the family was awake. How he did so you may indeed wonder, as at the many other ways in which his energy seems superhuman. Exceptionally strong he certainly was, and, being short, was not tired out as soon as he might have been had he had a taller frame to carry about. And, besides great energy, he was especially gifted with foresight in deciding what he could do well and what he could not, and what would appeal to him and what would not. Having enough self-assurance never on any account to waste time on things that did not appeal to him, but were merely conventional—like shaving and wearing collars and ties—he was up in ten minutes in the morning, while a conventionally dressed gentleman of his day usually spent three-quarters of an hour in a mahogany-cumbered dressing-room.

So he began his tapestry-weaving in May of '79. The design he first made was of great curling acanthus leaves, inter-woven with vines and flowers and birds. The tapestry was to be some eight feet across by six high. The vertical threads were stretched parallel from top to bottom of the loom, so close as to seem almost like a sheet of material. On these the design was traced, and in and out of them he had to thread the horizontal wools, one beside another, as close as he could, taking different-coloured strands as he came to each change of colour in leaf or flower.

No wonder the work was long! Yet it was nearly half done as he rose one brilliant July morning, while the little clouds that dappled the sky were still rose and golden, and in the loftiest spaces of blue over to the west a few little stars were still a-twinkle. So fresh it was! The cool, quiet beginning that promised a jewel of summer days. And, though it was

London, the air was not yet dusty with the stir of the city, and was little fouled as yet with the smoke that would soon be pouring from numberless chimneys.

As he splashed in his Philip Webb basin, and pulled on his blue cotton shirt and easy suit of soft dark blue cloth, his thoughts were of Kelmscott; and as he settled down to work he began to plan how the day would be spent if he were there. Why, the mulberries would be ripening, and the yellow buds of the tiger-lilies would be turning red, and Faffnir [1] would be sprouting, and blackbirds and doves would be sounding their loudest!

But never mind—the garden here after all had strawberries just the same, and here just the same, and not so very much muddier at this time of year, was his beloved river!

So he settled down to his weaving, sitting behind the transparent warp, and peering through into the little mirror to see the front of the growing area that his needle was ' painting.' Already the leaves seemed to be alive and waving on the summer wind! Oh, lovely world of leaves and bird songs and caressing winds! Lovely no less in winter, when the winds bore the snowflakes through branches seemingly lifeless, and sighing so mournfully, and only the robin had the heart to sing! Yet from lifeless branch and from bulb deep under the frozen earth such glorious flowers were to spring! First the aconites, then the snowdrops, then the whole race of unutter-ably beautiful things; through the glory of heavy-scented honeysuckle and ponderous dark red roses, till the fruiting time, when the hum of bees filled the air, and the pears grew golden-soft, weighing their branches down to the very earth! And then the autumn winds, the scattering of the golden leaves, amid the dreamy blue of the bonfire smoke! Then once again the snow!

How he loved it all! The life and the growth of it! He felt a part of it so much that he had little care for religion,

[1] His yew hedge, cut into the shape of the dragon Faffnir.

with its promised heavens far away from this earth. It was enough to adore the beauty of life itself, and, when one's time came, to return to earth as the fallen leaves return.

And soon Janey and the girls would be off to Kelmscott, and not long after he would follow them. All this smutty, noisy, vulgar town would then be forgotten!

He smiled and worked on busily, delighting to see the work he had always longed to do grow beneath his hands. Why, year after year of such work was before him! And how much more, and how much better would he do! If only fate gave him time, and if only Jenny got well! Why, then his cup of happiness *would* overflow! Already, but for that bitter measure, it was full!

So he mused, for an hour or more, till the last grape of one purple bunch was done, and a pink rose beside it begun. And all the time the reflected light rippled on the roller of the loom above him, as the waves ran sparkling by.

Then suddenly, tearing to bits the beauty of the quiet, pure air, rending his dreams of Kelmscott and his own happy life to come, came the scream and wail of the hooters from the factory over the river; summoning the people to work, commanding them pitilessly to come, and toil amid sunless squalor while the summer day passed by, and another day of life, that could have been sweet, was wasted—wasted in earning that which would scarcely keep them or their children fed, could scarcely pay for shelter and clothes, so that at best their lives were wretched and dirty beyond belief. "Yes, to work," those factory hooters seemed to wail, "till night falls, and then you may creep back to your squalor till another dawn calls you; and be glad if you get through the day without the sack, for others, hungrier even than you, are crowding to work for even smaller pay, lest they starve altogether!

"Yes, to work lest ye starve. No thought of whether you like the work or not, or the life or not, for you have no choice. No one cares whether you wish to be clean, to be healthy, to laugh, to learn, to love beauty, to rest, or in any way to show yourselves to be living men. For you work for the factory-owners, not for yourselves or one another; your lives are theirs, to make for them more riches than they can ever use, but must lavish instead on useless things that serve only to show you that they are rich, that they have power to steal your lives, to make you pine and starve serving them, until death sets you free!"

"Yet," Morris felt himself replying, "every man who goes miserably to work could be going with *joy*! I was *free* to choose the work I was born for. Therefore it is play to me—and so should it be for every one of these. How utterly *pitiful* it is! Such waste of lives that could be joyful and beautiful, every one! As is mine, simply because I was born rich and free! Wasted day after day, year after year, till something is done! Till the power is taken from the masters, whose riches no one but fools could want; till this dreadful contrast between rich and poor is swept away. How rich could the world be then—a world where each man does the work he is made for, and work becomes play, as it is with me! Or better than play, for it brings a sense of usefulness no play can give! Oh, how rich would such a world be! How *wealthy*, rather—wealthy in health, happiness, freedom, usefulness! Not rich in money and the power of man over man, class over class, or nation over nation! Things that begin in competition and end in wars! But wealthy in the things of the earth that *are* worth having: wealthy in *life* and in the love of men for one another! Wealthy for *all*! Riches and poverty gone, and in their place *Common-wealth*!"

It was not the first time that his Kelmscott dreamings had been suddenly replaced by such very different thoughts as these: more and more often, as the firm's growing trade gave promise of a comfortable, easy future, at Kelmscott itself perhaps, with only rare visits to London, some conscience in him made the joyful prospect seem wrong and selfish: so many others were wretched and without hope. Could he, knowing this, be at ease and happy till he had at least tried to better things? No, no! Rather than escape the reproaching sight of their misery, like other rich people with taste, let him give up all thought of himself. Die, rather, in the battle to give life to those who had never lived; for to die thus would be better than any selfish life he could gain for himself alone!

And the very herrings, so plump and silver on their dish between the steaming tea-urns and other shining covers, which he presently found waiting downstairs in the breakfast-room, seemed more than he deserved of the world's goodness while others were toiling in need.

Chapter 23

BY RIVER TO OXFORD

They deemed it good
That they should go unto a house that stood
On their chief river, so upon a day
With favouring wind and tide they took their way
Up the fair stream.

The Earthly Paradise

THE 10th of August that year had been the day finally
chosen on which the family and a few special friends
should begin their long-intended river journey up
to Kelmscott from the Hammersmith house. A capacious
rowing-boat, fitted with a small cabin, was hired, and amply
stored with cushions, rugs, pots, pans, and kettles, and plenty
of good fare, including a case of various wines. Morris and
Jenny went down on the eventful day to see their craft; it
was named the *Ark*, and certainly resembled the original in its
ample and ungainly proportions.

At 2.30 in the afternoon the party of seven went on board,
and were soon pulling slowly past Chiswick Eyot, their
journey begun. There were four men, to take turns at the
oars; Crom Price, de Morgan, Richard Grosvenor, and
Morris. As he pulled away rhythmically Morris noted with
intense pleasure his Jenny's happy, reposeful interest in all that
was seen and said, and almost felt that the other frantic stranger
she had at times suddenly become was only a horrible night-
mare of his own dreaming. The three of them, two buds as it
were on either side of a still fair lily flower, May, Jenny,
seventeen, eighteen, lightly dressed, and between them their

mother's dark hair and calmest of faces, long fingers laid idly in the lavender folds of her lap—these three were surely a proud possession to have. Better, whatever one *used* to feel, than a wilful, hot-tempered son! And he was swept with a rare flood of deep content.

Soon to their right the long façades of Hampton Court glowed wallflower-red through the trees, in brilliant late sun-light, as the *Ark* moved by. And six miles farther on it was moored at the first night's resting-place—Sunbury.

William and Crom slept on board, while the others lodged at a waterside inn. Morning showed the place to be as un-sightly as by starlight it had seemed romantic, and they left it without delay! Clouds covered yesterday's blue, making inter-mittent sunlight, very fine to see as it passed over the mountain-ous, tumbling willows that spread out over the water at Laleham, showing glimpses of stately old river-side houses in their well-tended grounds.

They had gained the bank of Runnymede by tea-time, and, landing, spread cups and saucers and cake-baskets out on the grassy bank. A row of white poplars grew along the slope opposite, and flung their image far down into the reflected sky below. The beauty of the place made them delay, so that the night's halting-place had to be changed, and at eight the broad grey towers of Windsor showed before them silver in the evening light, above their steep, roof-clustered height. The sight of it pleased them no less next morning, when Richard Grosvenor took them round Eton, telling of his own misdeeds there years before, and of Ruskin's wonderful lecture to the Literary and Scientific Society in the winter of '73. Rain fell as they were out on the playing-fields, and they hurried back to the *Ark*.

William cooked the lunch that day, and very well he did it, emerging at last triumphantly from the little glass-sided cabin, with a rich-steaming, fat-cheeked pot of chickens and vegetable attendants. To finish, there was fresh fruit and

Windsor maids of honour, marred only because they had to
be eaten rather quickly, being the envy of a host of invading
wasps.

The seven on board the *Ark* were somewhat disconcerted
when at Maidenhead they found themselves in the midst of a
gaily decked regatta, and had to travel the course alone between
crowded boats and banks, de Morgan plying desperately at
the oars, the others trying to seem unaware of countless staring
faces, bantering comments at their expense, and smothered
laughter.

By night-time they had passed through Marlow lock, despite
the darkness and the roaring Charybdis of a huge weir, to
land at last and retire—Janey and the girls to a small lodging
in the town, William and Crom to the sound of lapping water
close to their ears, the other two men to a noisy inn near by.

The next day's voyage brought them to rest at the village of
Sonning, after stopping to see what had once been a Gothic
monastery, noticed at once by Morris as he stood up in the
lock, and presently enthralling him with its uncertain history;
Lady Place it was called, now merely a farmhouse, where
monastic and Jacobean splendour had once stood.

At Sonning all but Morris went ashore to sleep. Next day,
at first in the fairest of weather, they passed on to where Morris
felt his beloved Thames became itself at last!

They glided between stretches of slightly undulating country,
pale from many days of beating sun. Small water-flowers in
plenty, pink, yellow, purple, white, blue, grew abundantly
along the waterside. Sometimes Jenny or May managed to
pick a flower or two in passing, and so gradually filled a small
lustred bowl which de Morgan had recently given to their
mother, while she reclined, perfectly at ease now, sowing a
wealth of similar flowers along the border of what was to be
an altar cloth for a famous Lady Chapel.

Wallingford, to which they came by early evening, seemed
far from the perfect end to such beauteous faring. But rooms

were found for those sleeping ashore, and then Jenny and May, to every one's astonishment, hired a boat, and rowed about till dinner.

The next day dawned, wet and grey from night rain, but, apart from being cool, remained fair. Morris was the cook again, and soon after lunch they were passing the Wittenham Clumps, and the airy, perpendicular windows of Dorchester Abbey. All was familiar ground now to Morris, and he sorrowed at every change—dykes wantonly half ploughed over, willows needlessly ill-treated; here a group of elms vanished, there a barn degraded with roof of flagrant iron.

In late twilight the *Ark* glided within sight of the spires of Oxford, rising in sombre outline against the fast-darkening sky, already alive with stars. After a peaceful night Janey took the train on to Kelmscott, leaving the others to follow by water in two smaller boats, the *Ark* remaining at Bossom's. The last and perhaps loveliest stage of the voyage was now to come, and they savoured the last twenty odd miles of country willingly slowly. Wytham's wooded slopes diminished to forget-me-not at their back, as field after field of bowed wheat-ears stood right up to the river banks, alternating with stretches of ripe mowing grass, richly flowered. In every tiny cottage garden orchard trees stood laden, dark with plums, or weighed with scarlet apples; cows stood shoulder-high in rushes where they grew aside from the river, in the tributary ditches between the fields.

Above New Bridge, in the heart of the Kelmscott country, they rested and dined for once at a place in keeping with its surroundings. Then on again through the darkening evening, past some late haymakers, busy gathering on to their punts the thick sedge grasses from low spits of flood land.

It was quite dark when their boats passed under Radcot bridge; then suddenly, as they were gliding past the willows by Eaton Hastings church, unseen but audibly rustling, a bright star shone out ahead, and swung to and fro steadily, and the weary travellers pulled eagerly towards it, for they guessed it must be faithful Charles, sent down to guide them in.

Presently, heads nodding with sleep, Jenny and May were being led along the ridged track, their father holding each with a strong arm; through the green door, up the flagged path, and —oh, gladdest sight!—into the shuttered and candle-lit dining-room, and their mother's welcoming embraces. And very soon afterwards, made drowsier still by their hot, frumenty drinks, upstairs they both stumbled, to their own welcoming beds.

"Janey, Janey! You have lighted up the old house like the Angel of Candles!" cried Morris admiringly. Then, leading her up to her pomegranate-patterned bedroom, he said, with a short sigh, "You see, as soon as the old house has me in its arms again, all other places and wishes melt away! Mind and heart, it claims them both for its own—and rightly, seeing its utter beauteous kindness to those who dwell therein! Good night, my Janey! You are its soul, my dear!"

They kissed and separated, Morris to melt presently into his old carved, coffer-ceiled, posted bed, and the sleep that he himself described as "taken in solid bars."

Chapter 24

MERTON ABBEY

"I see no smoke coming from the furnaces," said I.

"Smoke?" said Dick; "why should you see smoke?"

I held my tongue, and he went on: "It's a nice place inside, though as plain as you see outside. As to the crafts, throwing the clay must be jolly work: the glass-blowing is rather a sweltering job; but some folk like it very much indeed; and I don't much wonder: there is such a sense of power, when you have got deft in it, in dealing with the hot metal. It makes a lot of pleasant work," said he, smiling, "for however much care you take of such goods, break they will one day or another, so there is always plenty to do."

News from Nowhere

A YEAR had gone by, rich as ever with the countless fruits of his ceaseless imagination. Even though those other strange, insistent thoughts had occupied him also; while the flower patterns were wreathing over the paper in front of him he would have such long, silent arguments with himself, and lately it had become quite clear which self was winning, and would have the say with his life. But the firm was thriving apace! Orders tumbling over one another, for everything it could make, from wealthy clients from all over England, and now for the throne and reception-rooms of St James's Palace. "If only there were no such thing as conscience!" with its last breath the selfish self whispered. He could be looking forward to a sheltered life utterly perfect and secure, far away at Kelmscott. But there *was* conscience, and it appealed, too, to his old love of a conflict for a worthy cause.

But to return to the firm, and its new and beautiful workshops at Merton Abbey—and a promise given some weeks before to May.

Morris put aside his pencil and went down to breakfast. Reflections from the sunlit river shimmered up on the de Morgan china, the porridge spoons of Iceland silver, and his giant teacup standing beside the urn. Above the roofs opposite a perfect April sky rejoiced his eyes.

" May, you shall have your wish this very day, and come to Merton with me," he said, as she came in.

May kissed her father joyfully, and ran to change into a white muslin dress worthy of the day; and they were soon in the train, being borne along through outer London, and presently saw fresh fields on either side, hedgerows white with hawthorn.

Two hours after leaving Kelmscott House they were walking past the old church and vicarage of Merton, presently to enter the green carriage gates and the new home of the firm. Lilac was in flower, growing all around the ancient wooden build-ings, planted, perhaps, by those very Huguenot refugees who had built the place as the centre of a silk-weaving industry nearly two hundred years ago, making use of the river Wandle, as the present craftsmen were doing, its waters being specially suitable for madder dying.

From the top of one of the outer stairways a voice called out to them, and de Morgan descended carefully, bearing a large bowl painted with peacock-coloured flowers, and ready for a second firing in the kilns he had built near by.[1]

May left them to talk, and wandered off to the chintz-printing room, to see if her own honeysuckle design had been printed yet. She was told its turn had not yet come, but they showed her three new patterns of her father's, called each after one of his favourite rivers, Evenlode, Windrush, and Lea, and as beautifully flowered as the banks of any of these.

So she returned to tell him, and presently he took her to

[1] But soon to be abandoned as being too far from his Battersea studio.

the dye-house, where an indigo vat, set in the floor, six feet across and deeper still, was just about to ferment, and would soon be ready for use. Morris leaned down and dipped his fingers into the seething liquid; then he sniffed the vapours.

" She'll be ready in ten minutes, Smith. Have you your hanks all weighed? That's good, Smith. Specially fine wool, this last lot from the North—ought to suit her blue ladyship this time! My eye!" he exclaimed, turning to George Wardle, who had just come in. " Those old French master dyers would have laughed to see the way we have blundered about for the last five years, with only an old herbal or two and our wits!"

" And the mind of a master-craftsman, sir," added Wardle. He was working manager at Merton, and a Faithful John to Morris. Many night-watches they had kept together by their first dye-vats, Morris in clogs and blouse, still stained from a recent course at the vats of Thomas Wardle at Leek, pacing the brink, alert for those first acrid vapours which mark the moment for action.

" If I am a master craftsman," Morris replied, " it's only after many years of slow, clumsy work, steady training of mind and hand; *glorious* work—the dullest of it—if you compare it to that being done for bare life by nearly all the other craftsmen in the world to-day, but still slow enough to put off those who choose it for easy work to be done while you gossip together— a fair wage for little work and much tongue-wagging, my merry men!" And he swung round on two of the new apprentices who were tomfooling and scuffling together behind him as he talked. " Get out of here!" he shouted, enraged at such insolent stupidity. " I'll not have rubbish among earnest craftsmen! Disturbing my other men, and treating this dye-house as if it was a back-street local! You've had time to see how heart as well as hand must go to the learning of all crafts— if you won't learn you can go to the devil! Go on—out, I say!" and he hurled a ledger he was holding at their heads, as they turned and fled from the place.

Morris ran his fingers through his hair several times, as if to soothe away his anger, then he turned to George Wardle, and after a few minutes' talk with him, and a final word to Smith, took May's arm, and they went out into the sunshine, and were soon talking gaily together, the storm quite forgotten.

They went under a wooden *porte-cochère*, and across one of the several small waterways that flowed close to the old buildings, and reached the one where the glass-painting was done; hung up in the windows were colour-charts, set with all the jewel-like coloured glass they could use; and, besides these, parts of actual windows waiting for some special colour to be fired, or for the face to be painted on by a master-hand. May's eyes pricked with tears as she stared up at the intense crimsons, violets, and blues—glowing in a fold of gently moving robe or a distant landscape, or deepest evening sky, or merely in a fragment held close to her eye, and flooding the whole work-shop with its hue.

"Remember those early windows of ours—those of them that you've seen?" asked her father, as they were walking away. "There's hardly a coloured piece in them I couldn't make ten times better to-day. It's like that with everything, though, I'm afraid! When you look back at early efforts you can't think *how* you can have been actually *proud* of them at the time! My wig, how pleased I was with *Guenevere*, when she first came out! Whereas now it makes me cross to think she's still at large, bearing my name and spouting all that moonshine!"

"Oh, Father, how can you talk so! But one should be sorry for you, I suppose, since you're the one person in the world not able properly to appreciate your books, or get the joy from them that others do. *I* love the *Guenevere* stories some of the *best*, just because they came from you as impulsively and easily as the song to the blackbird in April. That gives them a beauty all their own, and never to be got again, and balances their value with the very best you've written since—anyway, that's what I think!"

" Dear child, you're as unfit as I am to see and judge truly! But, to tell you a secret, I can't dislike those firstlings wholly myself, as long as they hold the memory of those summer days when I first knew your mother, as men know angels— being themselves unnoted. Now, we have strolled up and down this little Mesopotamia long enough, without noticing, either, much of the glimpses of river and trees and old roofs that can be seen from here, and talked enough about thoughts and feelings of twenty odd years back. Come, to the weaving, sheds! You can see the back of them across the water there."

Presently they were trying to talk above the rattling of many looms: some high-warp, some low-; some worked by clearly aged men, some by little more than boys. Over by one of the tall windows stood a high loom worked by a pale youth. With the quick, skilled movements of a practised hand, his fingers stitched at the web before him.

" That's young Dearle—you remember the little lad I taught on the second loom we had at Queen Square? Well, there he is, and one of our best weavers at the high-warp now!"

" Oh, he's doing Mr Crane's Goose Girl picture!" exclaimed May, delighted.

" Yes, and we're going to let him do the whole of it, face and all, this time."

They watched him for some moments, his mind clearly set on what he was doing, and then left him undisturbed. In another part, where lengths of fine white muslin were being woven, with a white pattern of one of Morris's flower designs, May found them actually at work making the snowy lengths she had asked for, for sun-curtains for the five long drawing-room windows at Hammersmith.

There was one more thing to be seen before they had tea, her father told her, and they went across to a small meadow, used as a rule for bleaching calico; but now it was occupied by an immense patterned carpet, just finished for Mr Howard's drawing-room at Naworth Castle. There it lay, finished at long last, put out to dry after its plunge in the Wandle, and almost covering the little meadow, which Morris had planted round with a circle of young poplar-trees.

May gasped at the size and beauty of it, and Morris could hardly conceal his own pride in the achievement, since only now, for the first time, was he seeing the carpet as a whole himself.

" It looks jolly enough, lying there sunning itself on our calico meadow! How to get it to Naworth is our next problem! It weighs about a ton, I should think! Howard had better send an elephant to carry it away—but come along, Maidie mine—it really is time for our tea! "

They found it already laid in Morris's own room, and while they drank it, and enjoyed the rich rice-cake May had brought from home, she asked about the various things she saw about the room. Up against the windows strips of dyed velvets were hung, to test if their colours faded to pleasant shades. On her chair-seat there was a piece of special brocade, being tried, as her father said, to see how it would stand up to backside-wear. All about the place there were boxes filled with newly dyed wools; dyed silks for damask-weaving, pieces of chintz, tracings, patterns for carpets on point paper— and so many things more she feared to exhaust him with her questions.

Up on one of the chests stood a large peacock de Morgan pitcher full of lilac, and May remembered that she had thought of taking back an armful to her mother, and that it would soon be time for them to start walking towards the station. So presently they both went out, Morris to have a further word with Wardle, May to gather as much lilac as she could in the meantime. By the time they had got to the station, and had found a carriage to themselves, the sun was shining low through the trees, and when they reached Hammersmith it was quite dark. At home they found Janey, sitting at an open window, working in a flood of candlelight on an embroidered cover for the carved bed at Kelmscott. Every flower from the garden was there, and round it ran the blue, winding river, with here and there a kingfisher, and in one corner the old house itself. As May arranged the lilac in the great Grès de Flandre pitcher, with its pattern of strange blue flowers and little leaping horses, she told her mother about the curious old workrooms she had seen, with their wooden buttresses and tall windows, and about the quite young boys and old men, all busy at some machine or manual work.

"And they all seem so fond of Father," she concluded. "Not that he spoils them, I'm sure, for I heard him speak quite sharply to two of the men in the dye-house for fooling about when he was giving instructions. But they all seem to like their work, and they certainly don't look like the usual factory workers—not worn to shadows through constant labour and lack—they look like men."

Such was Morris's life as he neared his fiftieth year—save for Jenny's illness, happier than he had ever hoped it would be. Yet it was this very happiness which drew him step by step into the struggle for social reform which was just then gathering force. By '83 he had become a militant Socialist, and the heroic struggle which took the best part of his energy for the next five years had begun in real earnest.

Chapter 25

WARRIOR BARD

Wake, London lads!
Chants for Socialists

"THERE he comes! Here's Comrade Morris! Hurrah for Morris!" shouted the excited crowd, as the wagon decked gaily with green boughs came swaying into view.

For the hardships of the workers under the present depression of trade had made many desperate with indignation and anxiety, not only of the poor themselves, but of those who strove to help them, and to lead them in their struggle for better treatment; and in the forefront of the would-be helpers was Morris himself. Thrilling it was to him to see the large,

139

orderly, yet determined crowd who were gathering to hear him. It seemed as if the people were coming to life at last, not in aimless anarchy, but in serious demand of their rights, which, if demanded strongly enough, could but be granted by their masters, who depended on their labour for every necessity of life itself! Oh, if only people would realize this! No anarchy was needed—if they would only *wake*, only become *men*, instead of less than men! Well, to-day, if ever, he'd have a chance to tell them. And his heart swelled with hope and joy as the wagon drew up, and the people fell silent to hear him speak.

" Working people of England," he began, " you who should be the wealthiest and most powerful of all classes of men! Wealthiest, because without your labour no wealth can be! Most powerful, because your class outnumbers all other grades of society together! To your labour the race of man owes the bread he eats, the clothes that warm him, the fires that cheer him, and the roof and walls that shelter him from the tempest and the snow! Without your labours kings—aye, emperors—must die of hunger and cold! Who is it dares oppress you, my friends?

" Oh, fellow working-men, can you tell me what it is that has happened? Can you answer me, if I ask why, instead of rich, you are poor? Why, instead of powerful and respected, you are oppressed and reviled? Can you tell me how it has happened that this very day, in this land of wealthy cities and fertile fields, many of you are hungry, many of you are home-less? Aye, and your wives and children hungry and home-less too!

" Hungry, in this city where on every side we see signs of luxury and plenty! Hungry, you who sowed the corn; homeless, you who builded these great houses; while all around you see luxury and plenty loaded without limit upon those who never sowed, never builded! Loaded on them far beyond any reasonable human want, so that they are surfeited

with luxuries which anyone worthy to be called a man must
spurn with utter contempt!

"Wealth is *yours*, by right of your labour! Will you let it
be stolen from you for ever? Will you stand helpless, looking
on on this monstrous theft, while you and your families are
hungry and cold? You the strong, the many, by whose labour
all men live!

"How long will you let them steal from you; steal, and
give nothing in return; nothing but leave to be their slaves, to
live that you may work for them, year after year, until you die?

"Oh, my dear friends, my fellow-men, do you not see the
power that is yours if you will but use it? The mighty and
invincible sword that lies ready to your hand, if you will but
grasp the hilt? The sword of unity, of fellowship of one man
for another, of common endeavour for the common good?

"You have only to stand together, firmly and without fear,
and no one can dare to oppose and revile you; as they will do
so long as you are like sheep that are scattered, which the wolf
devours unopposed!

"Have done with weeping like helpless children! Cease
quarrelling among yourselves like idle boys! Stand up like
men together and demand your just rights! Only stand
together and the victory is certain, for none can withstand you,
so united!

"You have borne it so long, my friends! Suffering pas-
sively, as if bound by some enchanter's spell! Perhaps you can
bear it yourselves, but look on your fellows—look on those
you love. Can you see them suffer while you do nothing to
protect them?

"I can lead you, and others of the so-called middle classes
are ready to do so, and to give up our very lives for you if
need be! But this is only a beginning! From among yourselves you must find leaders, from among yourselves men who
are awake, until you need leaders no longer, but all work
together, rejoicing in the power you have found, determined,

every one of you, never to be oppressed again, never again starved and cheated of the products of your labour! Determined to do without the so-called upper classes, who have so far battened upon you to such a dreadful extent! Determined to live, every one of you, and every one of your sons and daughters after you, a full and free and happy life! To sweep away riches and poverty, and live instead in Common Wealth and fellowship for one another!

"Do you know what life is? Why, I think some of you have forgotten! Do you know what it could be, and should be, for every one of you? That every one of you could have a comfortable, healthy, convenient, beautiful home, with the beauty and privacy of your own garden! That every one of you could live in certainty that your children could have the same, so that to have children became a joy, instead of the shame it so often is to-day, when they seem to be born to even worse poverty than were you yourselves!

"Security, freedom, friendliness for all other men, no more wars! Leisure, and happy work, amid the friendliness of the earth, and the beauty of its changing seasons, yourselves changing as they do: joyful and beautiful in your spring of youth; strong and helpful in the summer of manhood; leisured and secure in the autumn of old age; and when winter comes, happy as the fruit to fall, and the leaves to sleep under the snow, melting into the earth from which they came!"

His speech was broken by a fit of coughing, and he felt suddenly giddy and very tired, for had he not spoken thus over a hundred times in this one year? Spoken often to audiences of one or two, or against jeering, hostile ones, till his voice and body dropped with exhaustion, but never losing heart? As he stopped the people around had begun to cheer, and, taking the horses from between the shafts, began to draw the wagon themselves in triumphant procession along Park Lane. Morris's eyes watered and his heart was full of joy.

" They've understood at last," he whispered to May, who sat beside him taking notes, and was now pouring out a cup of brandy. But before taking it he rose once more to acknowledge the cheering, and waved his hat to the people he loved so much and longed so earnestly to help.

As he waved, smiling for joy, a tall, red-bearded young man leapt up on to the wagon and grasped his hand, congratulating him in an Irish voice. It was a new friend of May's, Shaw by name. Morris smiled again, as up came another friend and another. John Burns, later a Socialist M.P., was there, young but bearded; and a thin, distinguished youth, with lively eyes and hair on end—Robert Cunninghame Graham, already an ardent champion of the poor, and later to serve a prison sentence for his pains. A spare young Scotch man, with long chin and lean face, MacDonald by name, come down from Lossiemouth to earn a living as a clerk, realized that day his calling, and, throughout the long years of strife that were to follow for him, never lost sight of the ideals spoken by Morris on that hopeful day.

The cheering went on, and Morris waved his hat once more, then, turning to where Charles Faulkner, with earnest, eager face blushing with pride for his friend's sake, was coming to clasp his hands, felt the whole world go dark, and fainted instead into his arms.

Chapter 26

THE CAUSE

It is a dream, you may say, of what has never been and never will be: True, it has never been, and therefore, since the world is alive and moving yet, my hope is the greater that it one day will be: true, it is a dream; but dreams have before now come about of things so good and necessary to us, that we scarcely think of them more than of the daylight, though once people had to live without them, even without the hope of them.

Anyhow, dream as it is, I pray you pardon me for setting it before you, for it lies at the bottom of all my work in the Decorative Arts, nor will it ever be out of my thoughts.

Lecture : "The Lesser Arts"

SUCH had been the hopeful beginnings that gave Morris the courage to throw himself heart and soul into the movement that seemed to promise so much. Leisure, wealth, freedom, even art, even life itself—none seemed too much to give up if men were going to wake, if the oppressed masses were going to realize at last that the power to change things was in their own hands only! To realize their strength at last, and use it to demand what was theirs by right! It all seemed so clear to his straightforward and independent mind. Surely people would act as soon as he made it clear to them? He knew so well that there was room in the world to grow enough food for every one to have enough to eat, and that the work necessary to provide mankind with all the true needs of life—especially when the almost miraculous power of machinery was brought properly into use—was so small that in the leisure left people would naturally turn to some kind of self-expression to show how much they loved their lives—to art. So easy it seemed for a race of *real* men to live such a gloriously full and happy life, and never to sink down again into the state of moral weakness which would enable an unscrupulous few to exploit them and turn them into something lower than any animal! So easy it seemed for the world to right itself; and when it had, and not before, he knew well, would the taste of the world become right too, ugliness vanishing with the unhappiness that caused it, and beauty coming back not as a quality sought only by artists, but as the expression, visible everywhere, of the world's regained happiness!

But he had not reckoned with the subtle forces which make for wrong in the world—the incurable weakness and gullibility of the many, and the vastness of the psychological power by which a few master-minds can control them, for good sometimes, but so much more often for evil. Nor had his simple and unselfish heart foreseen the quarrels and petty intrigues which began to undermine the newly formed Socialist band as soon as it had started to gather strength. Not till nearly ten years had gone by, and he had lavished for the Cause health and strength which he could never regain, did he give up his cherished hope of some great change for the better taking place within his own lifetime. Only when every effort and all sacrifices had been made did he give up this immediate hope, and resign himself to being a pioneer merely of a movement the fulfilment of which he would never see. But with this at last he contented himself, and his aim was thenceforth expressed in the words " Make Socialists "— " Spread your views, and find your reward in the hopeful vision only of the change that must one day come."

During his career as a Socialist he had learnt to control his habitually violent temper, and had become instead exceedingly mild and tolerant, for the quarrels of his fellow-Socialists had seemed to him the worst possible thing for the Cause, and he had had to work his very hardest to get people to pull together. In '83 he had helped to found the Democratic

Federation, and had spared neither time nor money in its service. But after a year the continual cat-and-dog fights of his firebrand fellows made him decide to leave it and form another group—the Socialist League. For this he financed a periodical, *The Commonweal*, and wrote for it many of his Socialist poems, and his *Dream of John Ball*, telling of the Peasants' Revolt in the Middle Ages, which endeavoured to spread, with their strong words and level-headed arguments, the message of the Cause. But before long the men with whom Morris tried so hard to co-operate became impossible, crying out, as short-sighted anarchists do, for measures which could only do their cause harm—among others the use, in Guy Fawkes' manner, of dynamite. Two of them went to prison, and *The Commonweal* broke up, but with untiring spirit Morris formed yet a third group, the Hammersmith Socialist Society. This consisted of the most serious and clear-headed Socialists of his day, who met once a week at Kelmscott House for the rest of Morris's lifetime.

And so, having done his best in the world of active politics, Morris returned slowly to the artistic work which he so truly loved, and wherein his unique genius truly lay.

Yet, though the Cause had been his first consideration for six or seven years, he had nevertheless, with an energy almost. miraculous, kept his other activities alive. The firm, of course, had to be kept going, being his and his family's living; but his writing too went on, in the intervals between his speeches, demonstrations, lectures, and the long, exhausting journeys which these often entailed. This writing was mostly in the service of the Cause. Besides his *John Ball*, published in '86, he summed up, in '90, his politico-social ideals in *News from Nowhere*, a story as rich in romance and beauty as in sound ideas and level reasonings, clearly and impartially set down. The characters in the story, including Morris himself, who are placed in that future time when, he trusted, the world's worst wrongs would have been righted, make just such a voyage up the Thames as he had made ten years before; which gives the reader who follows them a capital chance of seeing the conditions of his Utopia, both in town and country. The best-known passage is that where the travellers reach Kelmscott, finding that, in a world altered beyond recognition for the better, his own home, being perfect already, is unchanged.

His essays too were many, and some of their titles—*A Factory as it might be, Useful Work versus Useless Toil*—show the message that is in them. Many too were his propagandist poems, best known being the volume entitled *Chants for Socialists*, most beautiful, perhaps, being the poem *The Message of the March Wind*.

And yet still more! In '87 he published his verse translation of the *Odyssey*, later of the *Iliad* and the *Æneid*.

As he sat in the train one day in '86, on his way to speak at Arbroath for the Cause, it was the text of the last book of the *Æneid*, and his manuscript notebook, that lay beside his lunch in his satchel. While he ate his cold chicken sand-wiches, apples, and cheese, and drank his flask of Moselle, he strove to think of his poetry—to rest his mind from politics before the trial of this evening. Outside the landscape swept by—grey, empty country, like that perhaps around Troy! And those smoking chimneys, with furnaces brightening in the heavy-clouded day, not unlike its towers, blackened at last by the final fire!

After lunch he filled a pipe with Latakia, and when it was well alight opened text and notebook, and began the work which soothed and calmed him more than idleness could do. His pencil moved swiftly, and when he paused to think it still moved, as he traced, half unconsciously, sketches of flowers and leaves along the margins, as in some illuminated book.

Half-way through the journey a stout old bishop entered his hitherto empty carriage, and after a doubtful glance at Morris decided that he was not an anarchist, but only a poet, and sat down before him, studying with deep wonder, over his newspaper, the strange person who was scribbling away as if his life depended on it, without ever a glance up. Yet the scribbler had time to look up too, for in his margin grew the bishop's likeness, though in abbot's dress, which so much delighted those who were to find it years afterwards.

Chapter 27

THE BRIAR ROSE

The Briarwood
The fateful slumber floats and flows
About the tangle of the rose;
But lo! the fated hand and heart
To rend the slumberous curse apart!

The Council Room
The threat of war, the hope of peace,
The Kingdom's peril and increase
Sleep on and bide the latter day,
When fate shall take her chain away.

The Garden Court
The maiden pleasance of the land
Knoweth no stir of voice or hand,
No cup the sleeping waters fill,
The restless shuttle lieth still.

The Rosebower
Here lies the hoarded love, the key
To all the treasure that shall be;
Come fated hand the gift to take,
And smite this sleeping world awake.

For the Briar Rose

ONE morning in the late summer of 1890 Morris had
as usual walked over to the Grange, to breakfast with
the Burne-Joneses; and as he and Ned sat afterwards
in the garden he brought out a matchbox full of the designs
for printing type which he had lately begun to make. For
he had never given up hope of producing books perfectly
bound, printed, and illustrated, as he knew so well he could

149

do, given the opportunity. And gradually the hope which he and Burne-Jones had so often discussed was coming true; not without difficulty, for Morris would not take up the craft of printing, any more than that of weaving, till he understood it thoroughly himself. But now at last his set of designs for all the alphabet was complete; a hand printing-press had been bought, and soon the actual printing would begin.

To Morris the best book in the world had always been the works of Chaucer, the writer in whom, he held, both the poetry and the prose of the Middle Ages had reached the highest state of romantic beauty, graceful simplicity, and easy dignity.

" I should like to print the perfect Chaucer before I die," he said, " and, of course, I can't do that unless you do the illustrations. The type and the borders I can do, but none but you, Ned, can do the pictures. So promise me you will?"

And Burne-Jones, who had always shared his love of Chaucer, agreed gladly. He would do perhaps as many as a hundred drawings, to be cut on wood, if possible by Morris himself, who had for some years now been a skilled wood-engraver. " Every page," said Morris, " must be perfect, and every letter too. Oh, how I long to see it—I can picture it all so well already! I can see your pictures, Ned—the perfect fairy-tale pictures, such as were never done before. Every page shall have a border rich with flowers—it will look like a painted book—like the ones we used to love so at Oxford. Ah, well, in time we shall see it! But now, Ned, you said *you* had something to show *me*—how selfish of me to go on so! Come, what is it? Not the Briar Rose *finished*, surely?"

Burne-Jones smiled softly, and, rising, led the way through the house towards the studio, where his newly finished paint-ings stood—the masterpiece of his life—the series of four large paintings on the legend of the Briar Rose (or, as some call her, the Sleeping Beauty). Still with his shy smile he ushered Morris in, and they sat and smoked before each one in turn, as he told him—as he would have told no one else on earth—

of all the thoughts and feelings, poetry, romance, and mystery which he had striven with all his great art to express there. And his art was great indeed. Never before, Morris thought, had the spirit of sleep been so perfectly expressed; never in picture, poem, or in music either. And yet the mysterious sense of expectation of something wonderful and unknown that hung over all! How it made one long—almost ache—for the fated kiss that soon must wake those whom magic had kept dreaming for just on a hundred years! And, oh, the magic, the mystery, of those dreaming faces—the king on his throne, and the wise men lying beside him! And the princess herself—never was youthful simplicity and loveliness so enchantingly seen! Why, her slumber and that of the lovely girls around her, whose pale amber feet were reflected in the floor of polished gold, made one almost afraid to breathe.

"I want you to write a verse for each one, Topsy—so will you?"

"Yes, Ned, I'll do my best, but nothing could be good enough for these. Oh, Ned, to think if we hadn't been at Exeter we might never have met! I should have missed the only friend in the world who feels beauty as I do! And Heaven knows what would have become of me then!"

"I often wonder what would have become of *me*! Why, without your poetry how much poorer would my pictures have been!"

"And my poetry without your pictures! Well, Ned, we've been lucky dogs, both of us."

Just then Mrs Burne-Jones, or Georgie, as she was called, came to join them, and the three went out and walked happily up and down the garden. Georgie was a great friend of Morris's, and was the most understanding woman he knew in matters of art; and the three talked long and a little sadly of the past which they had shared together—since Red House days! So much beauty they had known, and so much happiness; even if life ended now they could but be content.

" Why, now the Briar Rose is done, I feel as if I could go to bed like a happy child," said Burne-Jones.

" No, Ned, you've to do the Chaucer yet, and after that so much more! I'm afraid life will never be long enough for me!"

" And yet I'm sure it will be, Topsy," said Georgie, " for no one dies before his day, you know."

" Well, I suppose you're right," he answered, " but I shall love my life to the very end, I know."

Chapter 28

RETURN TO ROMANCE

Dreamer of dreams, born out of my due time,
Why should I strive to set the crooked straight?

The Earthly Paradise

NEVER had the room seemed so still, its white panelling
so cool. Morris was writing at the round Webb table
of pale rough-grained oak.

And now he looked, and saw that she had in her hand a book,
covered outside with gold and gems, even as he saw it in the orchard.

153

close aforetime: and he beheld her face that it was no longer the face
of one sick with sorrow; but glad and clear and more beauteous.

Now she opened the book and held it before Hallblithe and turned
the leaves so that he might see them clearly; and therein were woods
and castles painted, and burning mountains, and the wall of the
world, and kings upon their thrones, and fair women and warriors,
all most lovely to behold, even as he had seen it aforetime in the
orchard when he lay lurking amid the leaves of the bay tree.

So at last she came to the place in the book wherein was painted
Hallblithe's own image over against the image of the Hostage, and
he looked therein and longed. But she turned the leaf, and, lo! on
one side the Hostage again, standing in a fair garden of the spring
with the lilies all about her feet, and behind her the walls of a house,
grey, ancient, and lovely.

As he penned the last words Morris looked up, and out
between the high, white mullions before him, and over stone
transom and distant elm/tops, into the depths of shower/swept
blue. Yet again the sweet spring/tide, and surely come back
this year to find a change in his heart! He had slipped away
to Kelmscott to be alone with the old place for a while, and
continue a new story—first/fruits of this change, which had
already been shown in *The House of the Wolfings*, written and
published the year before. Returning the goose/feather to its
stand in the pewter inkwell, he went out. He had been
writing ever since earliest dawn had flooded in at the four tall
lights of the east window; now sunshine sparkled on all the
lawns, and glanced through budding branches, making this
garden enchanted with light as the garden of story from which
his mind had but lately returned.

Just a week before there had been the sad ceremonies of
another birthday, endured with feigned unconcern. He was
now fifty/six. Very well, what years were still to come should
be like those first years of sweet, rich imaginings—should be
what had already started—a return to romance!

June saw *The Story of the Glittering Plain*, printed in *The
English Illustrated Magazine*, and the publication of *News from*

Nowhere, his dream-prophecy of some ideal future time, set in the transformed scenes of his own life. It had been Socialistic composition at its pleasantest, a relief from the increasingly irk-some editorship of the *Commonweal*, fast tending towards utter anarchism, and so given up by Morris as hopeless, in November, when it contained his last statement and appeal.

During all these political troubles and strivings the prepara-tions for founding his own printing-press went on ceaselessly. On the twelfth day of January next year it came into being, when the first press was set up in a cottage rented for it, in the Mall near Kelmscott House.

Three weeks later the first trial pages were being taken, and the new activity had begun in earnest. Throughout the next five years, in spite of persistent attacks of gout, and the com-mencement of the kidney disease, that had already begun, slowly but fatally, to sap away the very sources of his enormous energy, book followed book, at an almost desperate pace, from what soon became two presses in larger premises.

And, in spite, also, of all other demands on him, some new composition was always in process of being written, and borders and initials being drawn, mostly for the great Chaucer, soon to occupy both presses continuously for two years—a growing anxiety to him, as its progress seemed more and more to be a race against the fast-ebbing tides of his life. Try as he might, with all strength still remaining, to crowd each moment with something new-written or -designed, the silent foe worked on against him, and presently deprived him of the capacity for dreamless sleep; the healing draughts became difficult to achieve, and briefer far than of old.

And so the years gained way on that face and form so long impervious to signs of age, as those who loved him noticed with chagrin, as he entered his sixty-third year. In the early autumn of '95 Georgie went down to Kelmscott; it was to be her last time there with Janey and William. To her it was pitifully clear how the passing years, since other times spent there together, had changed and defeated the three of them, while the garden had grown more lovely, filling year by year with increase of flowers and foliage, birds and fruits, as their mortal frames were steadily wearing away, and poor Topsy's most of all. Such were her thoughts, as she sat writing to her husband, in late sunlight, under the ancient mulberry-tree.

"I feel the added years in Janey and Topsy and me, so it seems like visiting something which is not quite real."

Tears filled her eyes involuntarily as she glanced across at Janey and William, pacing slowly side by side on the orchard lawn. The shadows deepened in the heart-shaped foliage above her, sending her in to finish writing by candlelight; while the two continued their slow pacing, until they were melded with the shades. If sleep would not come, it might at least soothe his restless thoughts, Janey felt, to walk silently like this with her in the cool garden; otherwise, he would be drawing or writing till late, and again before dawn, and never rest his mind. Oh, these sleepless nights! She had to watch them wearing him away! Sad thoughts were passing in William's mind also—but they were concerned with late battles over spoiled countryside, against wanton insensitiveness, until he began to despair of anything but the worsening of the world, and at last to wish he had never been born with a love of romance and beauty in such a heartless age. His hand stroked the unseen yew hedge as they turned to re-enter the house; the tiny fir-tree shoots must soon be clipped again, and this year the clipping of Faffnir, until now his autumn diversion, would be done by another hand, for it was now beyond his strength—as their days of fishing must soon be too, whatever old Ellis might say—waning, weakening—oh, why *this*, hardest of endings, to bear?

Back at Hammersmith, however, such thoughts were quickly dispelled by an offer from Burne-Jones to do twenty-five illustrations for a new edition of *Sigurd the Volsung*. With a rush of his old enthusiasm Morris wrote back at once: " I am afire to see the new designs, which I have no doubt will do—as to the age, that be blowed ! "

And so through the winter and following spring many distractions besides his creative work came to fend off gloomy thoughts—lectures on Socialism, architecture, " Anti-Scrape " [1] —and then there was the continual acquisition of more painted manuscripts. For several years now he had been unable to resist buying any fine old book that came his way. What with Bible, Psalters, Books of Hours, his collection already totalled eighty-two manuscripts. And so, though the Easter holidays of '96 caused him to groan of them as " four mouldy Sundays in a mouldy row, the Press shut and Chaucer at a standstill," immediately his despondency was vanquished by the news that a twelfth-century English bestiary, enriched with over a hundred miniatures, was being offered for sale by a Mr Rosenthal in Munich. Mr S. C. Cockerell,[2] who had lately come to assist Morris with the secretarial work of the Press, was dispatched at once to get it at almost any price.

Down at Kelmscott for a brief interlude Morris eased his impatience with contemplating the April loveliness that filled every part of the garden to overflowing with budding leaves and flowers. He had just stooped to smell a cluster of newly opened narcissi, when a voice hailed him joyfully, and, lo! there was Cockerell, hurrying across the lawn with a small parcel in his hands.

" You got it ! Oh, bless you—bless you ! Don't tell me what it cost—all I want is a sight of the creature—to know if all they said was true." Cockerell's white silk handkerchief was spread on the grass, and there beneath the blossoming apple-trees Morris beheld a most perfectly painted manuscript, lavished, page after page, with exquisite jewel-like miniatures

[1] Society for the Protection of Ancient Buildings.
[2] Later Director of the Fitzwilliam Museum, and afterwards knighted.

of every kind of beast. He was lost in silent rapture over the sight; it far surpassed his highest hopes in richness of colour and embellishment. Certainly he had no cause to grumble at life, when it could bring to his hands beauties like this! And Hobbs *was* re-thatching his barns and sheds, after all their terror that he might use galvanized iron! And back in Hammersmith, Chaucer would be waiting, finished at last, in white pigskin and silver clasps, to welcome him on his return!

So he was able to take leave of Kelmscott this time with peaceful thoughts. It was looking its loveliest, as it lay before his eyes bathed in earliest sunlight, and he little guessed that this was to be the last sight he was to have of his Earthly Paradise.

Meanwhile, back in Hammersmith, less than a week later, as he had hoped, the first finished volumes of the Chaucer arrived from the binders, and one was sent at once to Burne-Jones, who, besides contributing eighty-seven pictures, had comforted and soothed his friend patiently during the five years of its creation. Again he was spared foreknowledge of the future, and began planning new publications, unaware of how brief a space of life remained to him.

Chapter 29

GÖTTERDÄMMERUNG

I dreamed that I was in a boat by myself again, floating in an almost landlocked bay of the northern sea, under a cliff of dark basalt.

The Story of the Unknown Church

MORRIS had spent the greater part of June at Folk‑stone, where it was hoped that the sea air might do him good, and, though he willingly sacrificed thus the holiday which he would so gladly have spent at Kelmscott, a month there made him scarcely perceptibly better. Yet, such was now the esteem of the medical men (who forty years before never thought of opening a sick‑room window) for sea air as a cure for everything, that his specialist persistently ordered him a sea voyage. Norway was suggested; and, though the kind of adventurous voyage that Morris would have found pleasure in was out of the question because of his weakness, he did his best to look forward to seeing a country that was new to him, and in its historic associations scarcely less rich than Iceland.

At first he feared that he might have to go alone, but at the last moment an old friend, the cheerful companion of former holidays, John Carruthers, found himself able to go with him, and on the 22nd of July they began the crossing of the North Sea together.

Their craft was an Orient liner, bound for Spitsbergen, where the best view of the solar eclipse of that year was to be had; and, except for a few scientists, their fellow-passengers were mostly tourists, of the idle wealthy class for which Morris felt much mingled dislike and pity. As he took his place in the crowded saloon for dinner that evening the waves were running high, but were little felt aboard the great steamer; indeed, every effort seemed to have been made to make one feel that one was not at sea at all. Palms and azaleas and fuchsias grew in great gold baskets about the place; plate-glass windows, with several layers of curtains, from lace to tasselled wool, shielded the smartly dressed company from every trace of sea-wind or spray. Even the rushing of the waves, which Morris had loved so much to hear when on shipboard, was drowned by an orchestra of piano and strings, which played one popular sentimental tune after another throughout dinner.

Opposite Morris and Carruthers sat a sleek clergyman—dean of some cathedral, it seemed—for he was soon chatting gaily of the new restorations to " his transept" which were going on at home. Morris groaned: he had fought so hard to save old buildings from the ruinous mercies of ' restoration,' yet with so little effect, it seemed. Still, he kept his temper, even when the dean's wife took advantage of the orchestra's playing a riotously loud piece of Strauss to lean forward and tell him confidentially how hard her husband had fought against some society of mad anarchists, who hated the splendid clean modern Gothic that was replacing the shabby old transept—even then Morris only laughed sadly at the hope-lessness of things !

As the dean's wife chatted on, Morris thought of the little *Diana*, which had borne him so bravely up and down the troughs of the thundering waves towards Iceland, twenty/five years ago. What joy every moment of that voyage had been! Ah, then the sea air really did do one good! But no grumb/ling; above all he *must* be patient, for had not Janey said, as he kissed her good/bye, that if he really tried to enjoy it, then he really would get well, and this he must do, or poor Faffnir's beard would never get shaved again! And the Press!

So he bore up as best he could, and, sure enough, as some days later they sailed up the firth towards Bergen, he really had begun to feel just a little more alive.

The morning was blue and windless, and he and Carruthers stood at the prow. They watched the rocks and islets go by till they lost count of them, and yet there were more without number ahead. And on every islet, and every peninsula of the mainland, the sweetest farmsteads met their eyes. Little houses of pinewood, roofed with wooden shingles, or with living turf bright with meadow flowers; and round about, wherever the rocks allowed it, the tiniest meadows had been tended, and here and there you could see the reapers at work, swinging their scythes, with little blades made especially for reaping between the boulders where the wild roses grew, wanton and delicate with their pale shell/pink flowers. How natural and simple it all was, this life in the light Northern summer, that was brief and clement as an English spring! And, indeed, the ice/fields far away, and the snow/drifts that lay gleaming in the rifts of even the nearest hills, showed how close the pitiless winter was, and its frozen, sunless days, when the stars twinkle at midday, as the sun shone at midnight now.

"Listen !" they both said suddenly; and both travellers held their breath, while suddenly, to their delighted ears, faint and far away, yet clear and unmistakable, through the lonely spaces of the windless Northern air, came the haunting note of the August cuckoo. For this most care/free of all travellers, which had sung its last in England nearly a month ago, and sought a cooler and clearer air, was there before them, and now had sung to welcome them! But, though he listened long, both this day and for days after, Morris never heard the cuckoo again.

At Bergen they went ashore, and great was their delight as they explored the old streets, where each little wooden house was painted its own pale colour—some palest lilac, some palest jade, some palest rose, some pure white—making them feel as if they were walking through some glacier cleft, among the pale, changing shades of the ice. Morris was, of course, too weak to see as much as he would have wished, yet he really did feel refreshed, as he went unwillingly aboard the stuffy luxury ship once more.

Though Carruthers was to go right on the Spitsbergen, Morris had decided to go ashore at Vadsö, staying there a week till the liner returned. Here he found rooms in a white house, round which orchard and meadow were pleasantly green. He spent his week quietly, doing a little walking, and reading when he was too tired. Unable to go far, he got to know the nearest country well, and grew especially fond of one orchard meadow, where he used to climb up from the pathway and sit on a smooth boulder, round which the hair-bells and wild roses grew, and the apples, hanging red-gold and ponderous along the bowed branches, made the place strangely to his mind.

One day when he sat gazing past the gold fruit, at the ice-fields that glittered far away, the bright sun vanished suddenly, and a dark mountain of cloud swept over the heavens, soaking everything with a torrent of rain and glittering hailstones. Morris sheltered beneath a little cliff of lichened rock till the deluge passed and the sun flashed out again, glittering on every rain-hung leaf and flower with indescribable brilliance.

As he went down the meadow a peasant girl passed him, a basket of pears on her head, bare-footed, her skin pale gold, her locks yet paler gold, and eyes as blue as hair-bells. She smiled as she passed, with rain-wet cheeks, and seemed for that instant to be the very soul of the sparkling, rain-wet meadow and orchard, which smiled and flashed with such infinite joy under the sun.

Gold fruits a-smile, blue flowers a-smile, jade fields a-smile —in all these the life of the earth shone out, perfect in health and beauty—and most of all in her, the most perfect fruit of all! Such was the race of man, such its fulfilment—to bloom as this girl did! No other end was needed—nothing beyond this. Here was the life he had sought to give to the hunger-pinched, dirty, and diseased millions in the ghastly factory-towns at home! Here in this simple meadow! Oh, if only they could see it! If *only* they could see it!

On the voyage home he went ashore once more, when the ship touched Stavanger, a little port, mostly of wooden houses, older and poorer, but not less beautiful, than those he had seen at Bergen. Here he walked up a little hill, and looked back to where the sun was setting over the western sea. Among the countless islands that lay to the west how golden-calm the waters were! And the islands seemed to go away for ever, over the horizon and round the curve of the world, till his gaze was lost in those slenderest cloud-isles, numberless too, floating above them, gold rank on rank, all now so brilliantly afire!

The beauty of the fleeting light seemed strangely sad, as Morris gazed—symbolic, as it were, of the sadness of all im-possible things, of all hopes that were never to be fulfilled! Would life slip away like this, he wondered, when the end at last came? Would it leave him with such an ache of the heart as he felt now, as the gold light faded so fast into grey, and the chill glitter of the stars began above him? Well, he would face it bravely, anyhow—bravely as he had tried to live. Though his bodily strength was gone, yet his spirit would always be strong, he hoped, till the very end.

Chapter 30

"ARE YOU TIRED YET?"

The Earth and the growth of it and the life of it; If I could but say or show how I love it!

News from Nowhere

O N August the 18th Morris was home again, no better, and so weak now from the diabetes that was secretly sapping away his strength that he could scarcely move, scarcely desire anything but the one thing he always desired— to be at Kelmscott. This, he knew, would cure him, if any, thing could; and if even this failed—well, he would die happily, in the place he loved most on earth.

But, alas, he was too weak even for this wish to be granted! And as he lay in bed in his London home he began to lose all hope of seeing the old manor house again, for it became clearer day by day that he was dying. Yet for six weeks longer he lay there, watching the rainbow lights that the passing ripples cast on the ceiling; thinking his thoughts, day by day, and night by night, all through September, his beard and hair snow, white, fading like a flower.

Many friends came to see him, but he soon grew too weak to talk to any for long. True, at times hope seemed to revive in him, and he would talk eagerly to Ellis of a new collection of Border ballads he would publish—for, of all poems, he felt the most lasting fondness for these. Or he would talk happily to Burne,Jones of the new *Morte d'Arthur* they would make together for the Kelmscott Press, which should eclipse even the Chaucer.

"And you'll do the drawings for it, won't you, Ned?

Promise me that?" And Burne-Jones promised, trying to keep back his own sorrow as best he could. For he was losing the best friend of his life—his other half, it seemed—and without him he wondered how he would ever get on. Yet he must do all he could to cheer Topsy, whose great tenderness of feeling, hidden so long, had now grown beyond his own control, so that his tears flowed as easily as a child's.

One day when Lady Burne-Jones [1] was with him, and something was said about the hard life of the poor, his eyes overflowed with tears, and she wept too to see him, lying so still and white on the pillow, his snowy hair and beard spread all around him, splendid as one of the old gods, yet lovable as a child always.

During these weeks his friends left nothing undone for his comfort. One after another, a famous library had sent to him its most priceless treasures of the illuminating art, which he valued above all others; and great was the joy they gave him, though he was too weak to look at any for more than a few minutes at a time.

He had always been called unmusical, but this was far from true, for he loved music, as he did the blackbird's notes, all his life long. But, lacking time among his other work to indulge this love, he had firmly put it aside, though never consciously for ever. And perhaps it was with some regret for chances missed that a few days before his death he requested to hear some of the older music he had always loved, and Mr Dolmetsch brought a pair of sixteenth-century virginals, to play to him in his bedroom.

The curtains of soft grey-blue tapestry were drawn close, and the firelit room seemed lapped in unearthly quiet, as the musician poised his hands for a moment over the gleaming keyboard of his little flower-painted instrument. Morris lay still as death, white on the white pillow, but his eyes full of expectancy of joy to come. Then suddenly the poised fingers

---

[1] Burne-Jones was made a baronet in '94.

sank, and the virginals began to ring, so faint at first the sound seemed but a whisper, yet clear as the ringing of a glass, and as sweet as the robin's note in the fading starlight of dawn. Involuntarily Morris cried out with happiness, though the effort hurt him, and his head fell back on the pillow, and he lay with shut eyes as the music rang on and on, flooding his heart with the same ineffable tenderness, forgotten and sup-pressed long year after year, that he had known that summer fifty years ago, when he first heard them sing in Marlborough chapel, " I waited for the Lord."

The piece was a pavan of William Byrd, written some three hundred years before, and had all the effortless majesty of the peacock, from which that dance took its name; and all the deep colours of its plumes seemed interwoven, unutterably richly, in those subtle webs of sound that flowed on and on from the hidden wires of the virginals, under the magic of the musician's fingers.

" Are you tired yet? " Mr Dolmetsch asked, when the pavan ended.

" No, go on, please, go on," Morris whispered. And again the webs of sound grew from the instrument, enchanting the firelit room, but by this time tenderly thoughtful as the cloud shadows that sail over summer seas.

With Morris dream followed dream, floating by in an end-less stream that cost no effort, but was comforting and happy as nothing he had ever known before. Death, he knew, was very near him, but he could not think of it as real. Rather it seemed to mean freedom from his poor, dying body; freedom to live where he would—in the trees and flowers and fields, in the clouds and rivers and seas, in the wind and rain and sun-shine and snow—to feel all the seasons, unburdened any longer with his body's weight—living instead in the changes of the year, as if he were their spirit, needing no other body but them.

Why, soon he *would* be at Kelmscott, seeing, feeling, know-ing, living it all, as he had never done before in human body.

Janey and the girls too he would watch over and care for, and those who lived in the old house after them. And, oh—unthought-of joy—he would see the time when the world would be happy and beautiful and free, as he had striven all his life to help it to be! Already he felt some of that future's joy—some of the joy which his work would give to those who would be free and happy then, though they themselves knew him not! What need of fame or of public acknowledgment! His joy was in the joy he had given only; in the knowledge that he had given to the world during his life no less of happiness, of life, than he had himself received! He wished for nothing more, no tombstone even, to show where his discarded earthly body lay, though he hoped it might lie at Kelmscott.

" Shall I stop now? " asked a voice; and he opened his eyes to see Dolmetsch anxiously bending over him. " Or would you like one more? "

" Thank you. But no more just now. My heart's so weak, you see, and I can't help the tears coming, though I'm not sad really, but happy. You've turned all my sadness and fear into joy. Ask Janey to come, will you? "

But Janey was there already, in the low armchair, covered with its blue tapestry of the cuckoos, beside his bed, and as he spoke she laid her cheek against his, so that her hair fell over the pillow, and pressed his hands in hers. She too felt strangely calm, for, though he was so soon to be gone from her, the time between now and when she too was freed to join him seemed easy to bear, because of the great happiness that that freedom was to bring.

So she held William's hand, while the fire burned red and low, and the candles went out one by one. Then in the silence she heard river waves lapping, and a wind rising in the elms outside, as if a storm were coming. But instead of uneasiness the sounds brought her comfort, for they seemed to be saying, " Have no fear; all is well. All is well; have no fear," in William's voice, over and over, till her head sank back against the tapestry birds, and she too slept beside him.

Chapter 31

NIGHT

Therefore they made
A bier of whitethorn boughs, and thereon laid
The dead man,
And, casting flowers and green leaves over him,
They bore him unto Corinth, where the folk,
When they knew all, into loud wailing broke,
Calling him mighty hero, crown of Kings.
                    The Life and Death of Jason

AFTER Mr Dolmetsch's visit, as if all further earthly
needs had melted away with the last sounds of that
ancient music, Morris lay, day by day, his head motion-
less upon the pillow, his eyes closed or gazing far away at
thoughts of forgotten times, his white locks, smoothed out by
Janey's gentle fingers, peaceful as the winter snow. She would
lean her cheek down to his, to catch the faint words of comfort
and gratitude which he tried to give her, for he had become
too weak to do more than whisper—though his thoughts were
vivid as ever, and more tender because of his weakness.

As dying men do, he pondered much on the life that was
about to close for ever—not with painful regret, but rather with
quiet joy that all had gone so well, so much better than his
highest hopes in youth. The happy surroundings of his childhood! His first days at Oxford, when the January snow made
all so enchantingly beautiful; the precious friendships he had
made there! The long garden in Holywell, that thunderous
summer evening, when Janey made his life no longer aimless
and empty, but as worth living as ever a life had been! Dear,
ancient Kelmscott, and all that its beauty had meant to him,

168

guiding him like a star through the intricate mazes of his middle life! All these blessings and so many more had been his, yet he felt he had given no less in return: his poetry and stories, Merton, his reform work—yes, the labourer had been worthy of his hire, and was ready, now it was evening, to pass to utter rest.

And peacefully, at last, his spirit did pass away, on one long, deep-drawn sigh of utter weariness, that third morning of October, just as pale sunlight gleamed out over the leaping waters and glittered on the heaps of fallen leaves. Below, the sunless garden was deep with tumbling masses of autumn flowers, all shades of gold and purple, the haunt of late bees and butterflies, weak and sleepy from the chill vapours and rainy warmth.

Three days after the blinds had been drawn down, two, dressed in black, came out, and silently gathered the flowers into great sheaves. The dim house was filled with bonfire scent of chrysanthemum and Michaelmas daisy, as Jenny and May waited silently with their mother in the great drawing-room, so strangely unlike itself, while the sound of slow and heavy steps passed downstairs—then they went down and entered one of the waiting carriages.

Amid the bewildering, clangorous turmoil of the great station at Paddington, the group of mourners with their sad burden passed through unobserved, to lay the coffin in a wreath-filled compartment of the Lechlade train, in the coach that had been engaged for the journey. Here they were joined by others, from Merton, Hammersmith, and many of the guilds and societies where Morris had been known and loved; from far and near they had come to honour his memory. Simple working-men most of them were, with an unshakable belief in all he had taught them, and now filled with an abysmal feeling of loss, their leader gone—yet stubbornly holding to their faith in his prophecies.

Leaning on the arm of Burne-Jones, with two or three close friends, Janey passed to one of the reserved compartments, followed by May, their spirits sustained by the tact and kindness of Mr Mackail, son-in-law of Burne-Jones, and a mourner too for Morris, whom he had long admired with youthful fervour. Next door he found a seat for himself, among half a dozen black-booted, silent disciples. Presently they were moving out of the grimy station.

For a while the silence remained unbroken, but as the train swayed along through wet, autumn pastures, by thinning woods and rain-filled rivulets, gradually, first one and then another, they began to talk, about this man who had striven for their rights, until their words of praise were eagerly taken up by one who was clearly not of their kind, though bound on the same journey of reverence; a man of unplaceable appearance, aristocratically wild, princely-mannered yet untamed, with a build strangely inadequate for his large, handsome head of unsmoothed hair.

" I share with you in honouring the mind, the godlike strength, the more than mortal achievement of this great man you call your leader. Wisely chosen! Never was there a more noble, generous heart! And to me he seemed of no accepted age or race: the last, perhaps, of some old, mighty line of Celts—warrior and bard as he was—certainly not of this sick, helpless people whom he pitied so and tried to rouse from misery's apathy."

" Have you been following him a long while, then, might I ask? " said a little Welshman in antiquated rusty black.

" In person, no—for my life has been a wild and wandering one—but throughout many years tales of him have reached me, and I have watched him wrestling with evil and envied him—myself having been born with a curse that allows no rest."

" Our Morris never rested neither. Did for hisself with overwork, so we heard say by one as works at 'is looms down Merton. None could ha' worked 'arder! "

A broad Lancashire voice took up the docker's words.

" 'Ard work? Yus! An' there's those as don't intend to see all go for nowt. He taught us; it's our job t' teach oothers. If we don't—well, blast us, for letting 'un kick t' bucket f' nowt, I say!"

Several voices murmured agreement, and the Welshman spoke again.

" Indeed and there'll be enough who knew of his ways to carry on. But mightn't the great and small be given a notion or two of who he was, this dear man we are following for the last time and all? Some comrade schooled enough might write down all he did and all he was. Then (God bless him!) he would not end with us or broken parties, but be living and working till the Cause was won!"

Thus they talked on, till the train began to slow down, and through the white smoke streaming wildly on the wet wind they saw that they were in the midst of a great plain, dark with sodden plough-fields and almost treeless, and bounded to the south by a faint line of grey hills. A sad place, a sad day, they thought, for a burial, and especially his—soaked landscape, wild, wet weather. Well, perhaps he would like these as much as any; it was as if the day was grieving for him.

Several tiny stations passed by, all alike with fret-edged, corrugated roofs and desolate settings. Then the train drew up at a larger station. They had reached Lechlade at last.

A stout, red-faced man in corduroy and gaiters, wearing a black neckerchief, and black braid round his old grey topper, came up to where Janey was standing with Burne-Jones, and touched his forehead to her.

" There's a clean farm-wagon, best 'un we c'd find, ma'am, waitin' ready outside—if you'd let 'em take the master to church so?"

Janey murmured that it had been kind of them to think of a carriage so suited to him. So the coffin was carried out and placed on the floor, which had been covered with moss and wands of pale willow leaves. It was a yellow wagon, with scarlet wheels, and had been wreathed all about with shoots of vine leaves. A young carter, also wearing black braid round his workaday felt, led the sturdy roan away, at a pace proper to the sombre journey they were making. Behind the wagon walked those who had come to pay homage to their leader, and behind the heads of the principal families in Kelmscott.

It was a slow, wind-blown procession, through the wet, winding lanes showered with fitful gusts of rain, that pattered down on the willow-wreathed piece of Turkish brocade that covered the coffin, and on the bent heads and toil-bowed shoulders, on scarlet-berried hedges and thin-leaved elms high above, until the puddles spread and deepened, and the swaying vine tendrils trembled continuously with great crystal drops.

At length the little grey bell-cot showed, and then the church itself between the trees; and presently the procession came up to the churchyard gate, the waiting groups of villagers hushing their talk as the coffin was raised on six strong shoulders and carried into the church. The vicar of Little Faringdon, who read the funeral service, had been a boy with Morris at Marlborough. Both music and prayers were of the simplest.

When the ceremony in the church was over the procession moved out again, and over the uneven grass, while the waiting groups of villagers kept utter silence, and beside the new-dug grave those whose grief was deepest stood. Only the sounds of softly falling rain and the tiny bright notes of a robin were heard, as the vicar began to read, with a slow, sad voice, the words, resounding in their solemnity and comfort, which have soothed desolate hearts for centuries: "I know that my Redeemer liveth . . ." To Janey the words brought infinite comfort, a sense of perfect, peaceful resignation. William was safe in God's keeping now. Whatever he had believed, his life had surely been a Christian one, and God would care most about that. Then one day soon she would go to him; life till then must be a time of patient prayer.

The coffin had been lowered down, and now Burne-Jones came forward to the edge of the grave: ". . . earth to earth, ashes to ashes, dust to dust . . ." With trembling hand and ashen face he scattered the earth three times into that dark hole. Part of his own life had been lowered with the coffin of his friend; henceforth he would be like a maimed man, unable to feel again deeply anything but his loss. " Oh, Topsy, Topsy! Why did you have to die! "

The service was over, a grey evening light falling, the church-yard empty and silent again, but for the great elms creaking and sighing in the gusts of wild wind and rain.

Chapter 32

DAWN

JANEY MORRIS lived on, spending her days between Hammersmith and Kelmscott, where she is remembered as a white-haired and beautiful old lady, whose existence gradually faded into a legend, until she died in 1914. Then Kelmscott Manor passed to May, and it became her home for the rest of her life. She treated it as a shrine of her father's work, which should encourage and inspire those who believed in and followed his teachings. Her life was very active, for she gave both her energy and her money unreservedly to the inseparable causes of art and Socialism. Her greatest sorrow, besides that which the growing ugliness and commercialism of the twentieth century caused her, was for poor Jenny, whose illness gained on her, ruining the life which had shown such great promise in the beginning.

When May died in 1938 she left the manor house to the University of Oxford, to be lived in and cared for by people who should truly understand Morris, and should themselves be artists and writers.

The firm of Morris and Co. continued until 1939. But without Morris's personality it had not grown, and it was felt that it could not face the restrictions and difficulties of the impending war, and the managers voluntarily wound it up. However, perhaps we shall see his lovely patterns again in the homes of the future, for which so many of us are longing, for the dies of the textiles were bought up for a mere hundred pounds by some one who was determined that a time should come when they should be printed again.

So we complete our story of William Morris. Of all the great lovers of life and its beauty surely none was ever more passionate, more sincere, than he! And good fortune allowed him fulfilment of his talents in a measure rarely given to men. It was the very contrast between his lot and that of the mass of mankind that smote his conscience, until he hurled himself into that struggle to help his fellow-men in which he gave so great a part of his time, his energy—his very life!

Yet before his giant strength was spent he had accomplished more of worth than a dozen men of talent put together. As artist he was beyond question the greatest designer ever known; his eight hundred patterns are rich not only in the taste and skill of the ancient Greeks and Persians, but in the romantic imagination which only the greatest English poets have pos-sessed. As a master craftsman he was without equal: he revived, one after another, those crafts of the hand which the cheap mass-production of the factories had all but slain. Printing of figured stuffs, dyeing, tapestry-weaving and carpet-weaving, glass-painting, book-printing—to name but a few of his activities—and in each one he found an artist-craftsman's pleasure, even to the very last. How intolerably it must have pained him, therefore, to know that millions of other men were wasting their lives in utterly joyless toil, slaves to the machines which had come into being that they might be slaves to man! And in his writings he was, in his own way, unsurpassed. In the haunting beauty of his imagery, and in his genius for touching the heart of his reader with that rare, indefinable magic, and melancholy, which is found only in the greatest and most thoughtful art in the world.

His theory of art was simple. He held art in any man-made thing to be nothing more nor less than the expression of the joy felt by him who made it. And similarly he saw in the beauty of the natural world the expression of the joy that God must have felt in creating it.

Morris stands apart from the insipid art of his own day in

splendid independence. And so must we, following his example to-day, especially since such dreadful evils have overtaken the world since his death.

During the years since the ending of the First World War commercialism and nationalism run wild have reduced men to something almost sub-human, so that they will fight for any political charlatan, spend their money on any rubbish that is sufficiently advertised, and gape like fools at any kind of freak art that is served up by entirely cynical dealers and Press. Both in art and in literature the very sewers have been dragged to produce the sensations that are imperative if people are to buy anything that is without any intrinsic value; and in this way fashion has followed fashion, each one worse than the last.

But this downhill race cannot last for ever, in politics, commerce, or art. The end must come, and is nearer than most dare to hope. For already the cry is heard everywhere from those who have, through bitter experience, come to their senses, " Give us bread instead of stones! " To-day, when public money is mis-spent by the guardians of our art galleries on worthless work, those who used to be completely taken in have now seen through the fraud, and are indignantly disgusted. Picasso no longer deceives even the fashionable fool or the pseudo-intellectual. But whenever a genuine artist dares to exhibit sincerely beautiful work, however much the critics may cry him down, he will be sold out. People are waking up!

Bitter fights there will be, we all know, against the ugliness and evil of present days, with the victory constantly shifting from side to side, but the main flood of the tide cannot be stayed, for mankind has woken and is coming into his own! And his splendid power will grow ever faster, until, when life is full, and joyful, and fruitful as the God Who created it surely meant it to be, then will the labours of William Morris and all the great humanitarians since the beginning of time be fulfilled.